1830

PRIVATE LAND CLAIMS IN EAST FLORIDA

REPORT NUMBER 25 TO THE 21ST CONGRESS FIRST SESSION
FROM THE SECRETARY OF THE TREASURY

U.S. CONGRESS

Heritage Books
2025

HERITAGE BOOKS
AN IMPRINT OF HERITAGE BOOKS, INC.

Books, CDs, and more—Worldwide

For our listing of thousands of titles see our website
at
www.HeritageBooks.com

A Facsimile Reprint
Published 2025 by
HERITAGE BOOKS, INC.
Publishing Division
5810 Ruatan Street
Berwyn Heights, MD 20740

Report No. 25 to the 21st Congress First Session
from the Secretary of the Treasury
1830

Previously published:
Institute of Historic Research
Signal Mountain, Tennessee

International Standard Book Number
Paperbound: 978-0-7884-9884-8

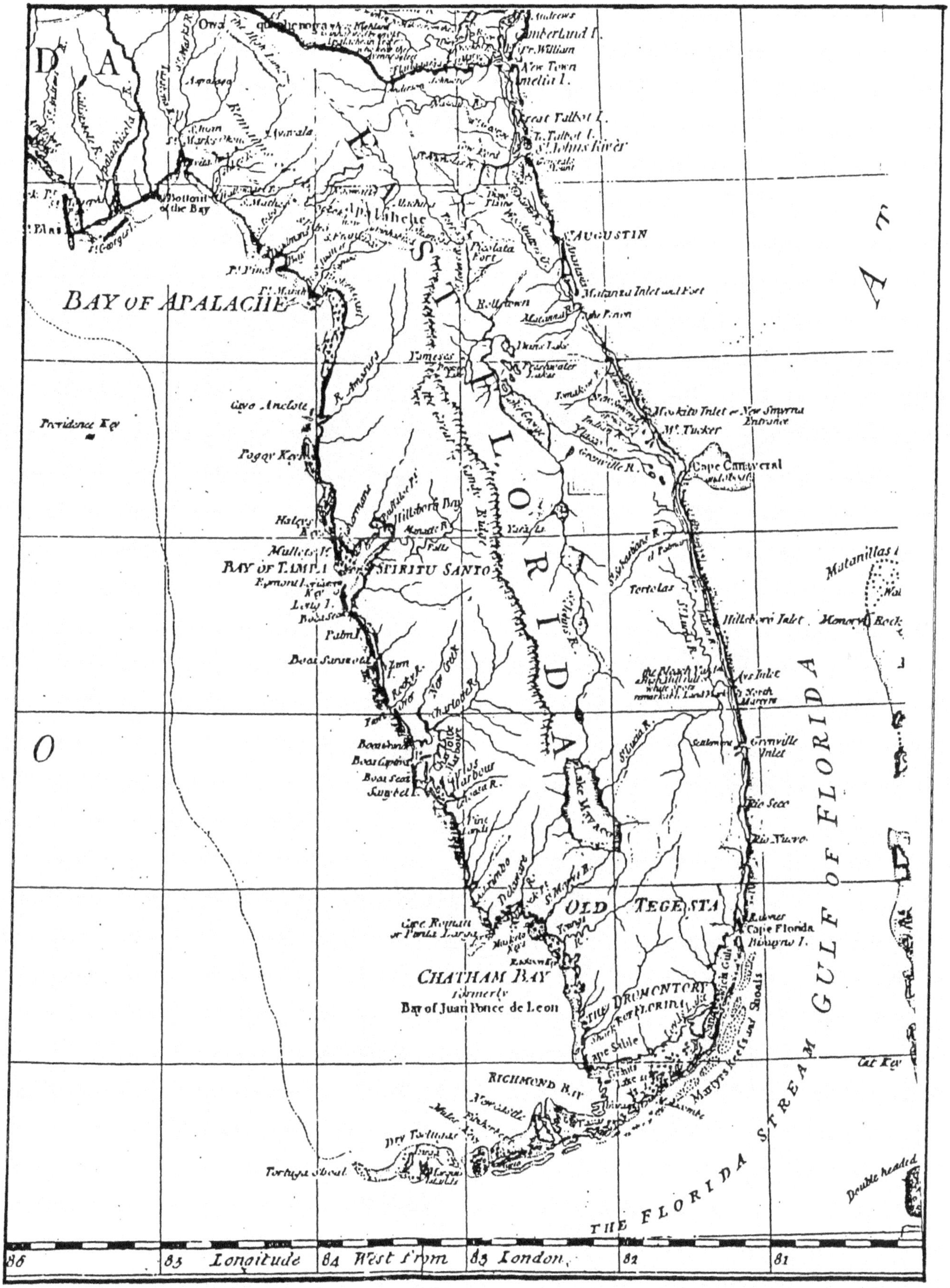

Detail of A NEW AND GENERAL MAP OF THE SOUTHERN DOMINIONS BELONGING TO THE UNITED STATES OF AMERICA by Laurie & Whittle 1794

REPORT

FROM

THE SECRETARY OF THE TREASURY,

With the final Report on Private Land Claims in East Florida, prepared by the Register and Receiver of that District, under the act of 23d May, 1828.

JANUARY 18, 1830.

Read, and ordered to be printed.

TREASURY DEPARTMENT,
January 14, 1830.

SIR: I have the honor to transmit a final Report on Private Land Claims in East Florida, prepared by the Register and Receiver of the district of East Florida, under the act of the 23d May, 1828, entitled "An act supplementary to the several acts providing for the settlement and confirmation of Private Land Claims in Florida."

I have the honor to be,
With high respect,
Your obedient servant,
S. D. INGHAM,
Secretary of the Treasury.

The Hon. the PRESIDENT
of the Senate of the U. S.

LAND OFFICE, ST. AUGUSTINE,
January, 1819.

The Hon. RICHARD RUSH,
Secretary of the Treasury:

SIR: In obedience to the law of 1828, we now transmit to you a final report on the Private Land Claims within this District.

We have adhered, throughout, to the principles of decision previously adopted and reported to Congress at its last session. We have become more and more confirmed in the opinion, that the positions laid down in that report are correct.

Previous to the years 1790 and '91, few, if any, lands had been granted in this District by the Spanish Government. It was on the 29th October, 1790, that the first royal order was issued from the Court of Madrid to the Governor of this Province, authorizing him to make grants of lands to a certain description of foreigners, and under certain conditions. This Royal order will be found in page 996 of the last volume of land laws. Although this order was intended to embrace the case of foreigners alone, yet, as it was more liberal in the quantity of land to be granted than the Royal order of 1756, page —— of same volume, or the laws of the Indies, it was invariably applied by the Governors of this Province to subjects as well as to strangers. Something was left to the discretion of the Governor, and it was his duty to exercise that discretion soundly, both as to the quantity of land to be granted, and the tenure by which it should be held. This was done by Governor Quesada, immediately upon the reception of the Royal order above alluded to, and as early as the 20th November, 1790.

By his regulations, page 997 of same volume, it will be seen that one hundred acres of land were allotted to each head of a family, and fifty acres to the other members. Thus it appears, that, no matter from what source may have emanated the limitation above mentioned, it is cotemporaneous with the order itself, and equally obligatory, until it should be repealed by competent authority.

So much for the quantity of land to which each applicant was entitled. Upon the subject of the ten years possession, necessary to complete the title, our predecessors in this office have alleged in their report that this was a regulation of Governor White. Upon a reference to the case of William H. G. Saunders, (Report 2, No. 111,) it will be seen that this is a mistake. In that case, on the 10th September, 1791, after having granted the land in perpetuity, the Governor has adopted the following language: "And finally, although this donation and concession is made in perpetuity, the donee, or his heirs, cannot alienate or transfer the said lands to any other owner, until the ten years' possession be passed; and even then, the first sale must be executed with permission of the Government, and in any other way it should be nulled," &c. He then adds, "Under the said conditions, and not without them, I cede, renounce, and transfer the said lands," &c.

This is one of the first grants made under the Royal order of 1790, dated less than one year after the reception of that order, and proving, as we think, conclusively, that this condition, attached to every grant, under that authority, is as old as the authority itself.

Upon every grant of lands made by the Spanish Governors, under the laws of the Indies, or the ordinances of the King, in this as in other provinces, some similar condition was imposed, varying only in its duration. By the laws of the Indies, if we remember correctly, before the title could be consummated, it was necessary that the grantee should prove four years' continued possession. By the regulations of O'Riley, Governor and Captain General of the Province of Louisiana, no lands granted could be sold until after three years' possession—and by those of Morales, this, together with additional conditions, was imposed upon the grantees. Perhaps a longer term of possession may have been required in this Province under the order of 1790, because that order applies solely to foreigners: and if the subjects of the King chose to obtain their lands under the same order, because of a larger quantity authorized thereby to be granted, it was but fair that the prolonged period of possession should attach likewise to them. It has been the policy of every Government, that possessed colonies abroad, to require of the grantees of land, some evidence that the application therefor was made, not for the purposes of speculation, but of agriculture. The British made no grants but to their own subjects, and invariably attached the condition of two years' continued possession.

Until the year 1790, so far as we have been enabled to discover, there seems to have been no power vested in the Spanish Governors of Provinces to make grants of land to any others than to native subjects. By the laws antecedent to that date, as we have just observed, three and four years of uninterrupted possession was required, on the part of the grantees, they being subjects only. Upon the reception of the order of 1798, Morales, the Governor of Louisiana, required that the new settlers who obtained lands under that order, somewhat similar to that of 1790, "should clear and put in cultivation, in three years, all the front of their concessions," &c. on the penalty of having the lands granted remitted to the domain; with the further condition, "That no person shall sell or dispose of the land so granted within the said term of three years." See articles 4th and 6th of his regulations, page 982 Land Laws. The regulations of Gayoso, of the year 1797, are nearly similar. Quesada, the Governor of the Province, very properly imagined, that a foreigner should give a stronger evidence of an intention to remain upon the land, than was required of a subject. For this reason, under the order of 1790, he required ten years of continued and uninterrupted possession before a full title was granted to the claimant. It is apparent, then, that, before a new-comer could obtain a grant or concession of lands in this province, he was obliged to take the oath of allegiance to the King, in the first place. Then, having discovered vacant lands which suited him, he presented a memorial to the Governor, in which he declared his intention to become a subject, and made known his wish to obtain lands, specifying the place at which they were situated. The Governor usually decreed the grant, leaving to the Surveyor, Don Pedro Marrot, to measure off to the applicant the number of acres to which he was entitled. By the fourth article of the instructions to Marrot, page 998, he was required to administer to all applicants an oath as to the number of their family, and then to survey to them the quantity of land to which they were entitled by the regulations of the 20th November, 1790. This being done, and the claimant having taken possession of his land, within from one to six months, as required by the grant, it was his duty to remain on the same for the ten years prescribed by the regulations; and if, within that period, he abandoned it, or sold it, without permission of the Government, it reverted to the Royal Domain. After ten years' possession, it was competent to him to prove before the Governor the performance of all these conditions, and to obtain a full and indefeasible title. He could then dispose of the land as he pleased.

The Royal Order of 1815 is the next general ordinance for the disposition of lands. Upon this we have already commented in our former report. It differs from the ordinance of 1790 in this: first, that the grant is made for services, and was intended as a reward or compensation for something already performed; and, secondly, it required no continued possession of ten years to vest in the grantee a perfect title. But, by the express provisions of the Royal Order of 1815, the quantity of land to be granted is the same as prescribed by the regulations of Quesada, to wit: "According to the number of the grantee's family." By reference to the case of Peter Meranda, on report 3, No. 17, our views upon the first decree of the Governor to the memorial of the applicant, and on the relative validity of concessions found in the Governor's and Escribano's offices may be seen. We have there said, that the memorial of the party, and the decree of the Governor thereon, found, as it usually was, in the office of the Governor's Secretary, passed no title to lands in the province. For example, A B would say to Governor White that he intended to bring in the province 100 negroes, and begged of his Excellency to concede to him 50,000 acres of land. The decree of the Governor in almost every instance was the same—"Let this land be granted to the applicant until, according to the number of his family, the quantity to which he is entitled shall be measured to him." This document, the memorial and decree aforesaid, was always thrown loosely about the office of the Governor's Secretary, and conveyed no title to the party. It was a bare permission to become a subject, and to complete the further conditions precedent to the grant.

A copy of this was usually given to the applicant, whose duty it was to present it to the Surveyor General, who, having administered the oath as to the number of his family, measured off the quantity allowed by law. To the case of Meranda we beg leave to refer for a fuller expression of our views upon this subject. Suffice it to say, that we have invariably required full proof of ten years of uninterrupted possession and cultivation, before we have confirmed a grant under the order of 1790, and some evidence of the previous existence of an original, as well as some probability upon the face of the paper and size of the grant, that the quantity conceded bore some proportion to the number of the applicant's family, before we have confirmed or recommended a grant, made for services since the order of 1815.

The British titles in East Florida are not involved in much confusion. By the treaty of 1783, and by the subsequent proclamation of the King of Spain, twenty-four months were given to British subjects to dispose of their property. By the Royal order of the 5th April, 1786, the King granted permission to all those British subjects, who still remained in the Province, to retain their lands on taking the oath of allegiance to Spain.

Governor Quesada, in what is called "The Edict of Good Government," article 4th, on the 2d September, 1790, after recapitulating a portion of the order of 1786, adds, "That all those that have not conformed, and do not conform, to the said conditions, within thirty days, positively should forfeit their lands." In addition to this, it was customary, and perhaps requisite, that the British grantees, upon taking the oath of allegiance, should present to the Governor their title, together with their survey, and cause them both to be recorded in the Escribano's office. When this was done their title was complete.

These, then: 1st, The grants for head rights, no matter under what law they were made; 2dly, The grants for services under the order of 1815; and, 3dly, The British grants legalized in pursuance of the Royal order of 1786, are the only grants within the Province of East Florida, the authority to make which can be traced to any law, ordinance, or decree, of the Spanish Government.

In adddition to the above, there are two species of grants, which perhaps may be valid, not from any specific authority in the Governors to make them, but from the general power with which they were vested to advance the interests of the Province. We mean, the Mill grants, and the grants for Cow pens. Of the first we have already expressed our opinion at large, in the report of the last session.

Of the second, the grants for Cow pens, it is probable that, after a continued cultivation of ten years, the party claiming may have become entitled to the land. In many cases of this kind, the Governor has given him a Royal title. This, perhaps, was a necessary inducement to the inhabitants to increase their stock of cattle, and thereby add to the wealth of the Province.

Upon proof to the Governor that a mill had been erected, we think it probable, that he had the power, in that case, without any positive law, to give a good title to the spot; not to 16,000 acres, but to the ground upon which the mill stood, embracing a quantity sufficiently large for all the purposes and conveniences of the mill aforesaid, with an additional privilege of cutting pine timber, either in the woods, or within the four miles square, or 16,000 acres, as may be specified in the grant itself. From the above remarks, it appears that all grants within the Territory of East Florida are good, which contain the above prescribed requisites.

1st, Under the order of 1790, when the claimant proves ten years of continued and uninterrupted possession;

2dly, Under the order of 1815, when it shall appear to have been fairly and honestly made for military services, and adhering, as to quantity, to the proportions made necessary under the regulations of Quesada;

3dly, British grants, recognised by the Spanish Government, according to the Royal order of 1786, and the regulations of Quesada, of 1790; and

4thly, and 5thly, The Mill grants, and Cow pen grants, with the limitations above specified.

We did intend to say something upon the subject of the Spanish surveys, from which we are now precluded by the want of time. We will simply remark, upon this subject, that the surveys made under the superintendence of Marrot are entitled to unlimited respect, and should, in every case, be regarded as conclusive of the boundaries. With regard to surveys made by private Surveyors, or Mr. Geo. I. F. Clarke, the public Surveyor, styling himself the Surveyor General, we entertain a widely different opinion. It will be seen, by reference to the instructions given to Mr. Clarke, page 1003, of Land Laws, that he is specially directed, "when called on by any person, to measure and bound lands to him, to require his title of property or grant from Government, that, on sight thereof, he may proceed to its measurement and demarcation." And yet, let it be remembered, that there is in this office a numerous class of claims, founded alone on the survey of George I. F. Clarke, measured without "a title of property, or grant from Government." He is further directed, in article 4th of his instructions, to conform himself to the directions given to Marrot, on the 24th October, 1791, and "to endeavor not in the front to exceed one-third part of all lands he should survey." He was directed to keep regular books, in which his surveys should be recorded; and yet, in his testimony, page 1014, he has declared, "that he kept no regular books of surveys since June or July, 1817, nor at any previous time." He has further said, that he possessed authority to survey lands, as Surveyor General, and no special order was necessary for him; and adds, "when the land was not specially designated, he would locate wherever the claimant pointed out, provided the place was vacant; and in cases where the land was specially located by the grant, he would, nevertheless, at the request of the grantee, locate it at any other place."

Throughout the whole of Mr. Clarke's testimony, he has expressly declared, that the instructions given to him, by the Governor, were not obeyed by him, and that he did not consider them obligatory upon him. That Mr. Clarke was honest in this opinion, we fully believe; but we cannot concur with him, and we consider every survey so made directly at war with the spirit and letter of his instructions, and, as such, entitled to no respect or consideration whatever. When Mr. Clarke was directed to survey by the grant, and when he tells us that he surveyed without reference thereto, at a place fifty, or a hundred miles off, we believe Mr. Clarke has exceeded his authority. When the grant contains one undivided portion of land, and Mr. Clarke has surveyed a part of it in one place, and a part in another, wherever a stick of live oak, or a foot of hammock could be found, the survey is not in accordance with "the title of property or the grant of the Government," and is therefore void.

When Mr. Clarke was directed to survey, to an applicant, four miles square of land in a body, and located a part of it in Alachua, a part on the St. Mary's, and a part on the Indian River, more than one hundred miles asunder, as was his custom, we humbly conceive Mr. Clarke has exceeded his authority. In a word, when, to an officer of the Government, written and positive instructions are given, prescribing his duties, and regulating the manner in which they should be performed, and when that officer, before a competent tribunal, has declared upon oath, that all of his official acts were performed without reference to those instructions, and in direct opposition to their mandates, we have no hesitation in declaring, that every such act of that officer is null and void, and unworthy of consideration. We have no hesitation in saying, that Mr. C. was bound to conform himself to his written instructions, as his sole guide in the surveys which he should make. That he was bound to measure to the claimant the lands at the place designated in the grant, and according to the boundaries (if any) therein specified.

That he had no authority to subdivide an integral grant, nor to change the location when once it was made; and yet, from the papers in this office, and from the express declarations of Mr. Clarke himself, it appears too plainly, that it was his constant practice to do all these. Wherever we have discovered a survey made at a place different from that specified in the grant, we have considered it our duty to look to the grant, and not to the survey, for the locality of the land. This has occurred in more instances than one, and we now remember two cases of 500 acres each, granted in Twelve Mile Swamp; and afterwards surveyed in Dirbins' Swamp, more than fifty miles distant. These lands were granted for services, and required no cultivation. We have confirmed them according to the grants, and not according to the surveys; and if there should be no vacant lands at the place specified in the grant, the claimants must lose them.

We have thought it our duty to make these few remarks on the subject of surveys, which will ultimately be found a most important branch of the adjudication of private land claims in East Florida. With these remarks, we beg leave, most respectfully, to submit to you, and through you, to Congress, the final result of our labors in this department.

We are, Sir, with much respect,
your obedient servants,
C. DOWNING, *Register.*
W. H. ALLEN, *Receiver.*

LAND OFFICE,
ST. AUGUSTINE, *January* 20, 1829.

SIR: We have the honor to transmit to you our final reports on the Land Claims in East Florida. We regret that this could not have been done at an earlier period; but, as the renewal of our commission did not reach us until the first of July last, and as the claimants before the Board were permitted by the law to introduce new testimony up to the first of December, we could not sooner perform the duties imposed upon us. Every claim has been now reported on; and, when the arduous duties which we had to perform are duly considered, we flatter ourselves we have not long exceeded the time necessary to complete them.

No. 1, containing seventy-seven cases, is a report of claims confirmed.

No. 2, one hundred and thirty-two cases, is a report on claims rejected.

No. 3, thirty-eight cases, is a report of claims exceeding 3,500 acres, the limit of our final jurisdiction.

Nos. 4, 5, 6, and 7, are reports on claims under the donation act of 1824.

No. 4, the first of donation claims, containing twelve cases, which have been confirmed.

No. 5, and second of donation claims, thirty-seven cases rejected.

No. 6, and third of donation claims filed subsequently to the first of November, 1827, containing seventeen cases, also rejected.

No. 7 and No. 4, of donation claims, containing four cases, recommended to Congress for confirmation.

No. 8, containing thirteen cases, is a report on, and an abstract of, British grants.

No. 9, is a list of twenty-one town lots, confirmed to the claimants.

No. 10 is a list of forty-nine town lots, in which there is no evidence of title, and which are rejected.

No. 11 contains a list of twenty claims, situated within 1,500 yards of the fortifications of this city, between the North and St. Sebastian's river, and held by the same tenure, viz. "That the party should settle on and possess the land until it should be reclaimed by the Government for military purposes." These claims we have no power to confirm; but for the reasons attached to the abstract, we have recommended them for confirmation.

No. 12 contains the cases of the Messrs. Clarkes, of this place, and those who claim under them. The cases are thirty in number.

We have thought it better to embrace these cases in a separate report and abstract, because they were more numerous than those claimed by any other individual, and because they involved more difficulty in their investigation and decision. Of these cases, No. 4, including 5, 6, and 7, is recommended to Congress for confirmation. No. 8, including 9, 10, and 11, is also recommended. No. 26, including 24 and 25, is recommended for confirmation. Nos. 14, 15, 16, 17, 18, and 19, have been confirmed. Nos. 12, 27, 28, and 29, are also confirmed. No. 3 is a part of a grant recommended by the former Board of Commissioners.

Nos. 1, 2, 21, 22, 23, and 30, are rejected.

No. 13, containing fifty-seven cases, is an abstract of claims, in which no title of property has been filed.

No. 14, two cases, is a report and abstract on conflicting British and Spanish grants

No. 15, containing sixteen cases of claims confirmed, and recommended for confirmation, by the Board of Land Commissioners, which were left out of their abstracts, and were returned to this Board by the Commissioner of the General Land Office for our report thereon.

No. 16 contains ——— cases, which were rejected by the former Board of Commissioners, and never reported to Congress.

We thought it our duty to supply this omission, that both Congress and the claimants might be apprised of the fate of all the claims filed before this Board.

In addition to this, Sir, we herewith transmit to you an alphabetical list of all the cases reported on during the present session. We believe it will greatly facilitate an examination of the abstracts and reports herewith sent, and enable a party at a glance of the eye to ascertain the fate of his claim. On this list, the first ruled column is the number of the report on which the claim will be found, and the second column contains the number of the claim upon that report. It will be seen, that, between the 1st of July, 1828, and January, 1829, a space of less than six months, we have decided, and finally reported on, nearly six hundred claims. To do this, and to meet the views of Congress, in bringing to a close the sittings of this Board, we have found it indispensably necessary to employ an additional clerk—the one allowed us by law being assiduously engaged in the translation of the Spanish documents before the Board.

To this clerk we have given a certified account of services rendered: and, although we were not by law authorized to employ him, yet, when it is considered, that, without his aid, the duties of the office could not have been performed, nor the decision of, and the report upon, the claims completed, we hope that his account may be allowed, and our necessary departure from the law in this single instance sanctioned by the proper authority.

In deciding upon the proper sum for his remuneration, we have had no guide but the law of 1825, allowing additional clerks to the former Board of Commissioners. By that we have been governed, as will be seen by the certified account.

With these remarks, we have the honor to submit to you the accompanying documents.

We are, Sir, with much respect,
Your most obedient servants,
C. DOWNING, *Register.*
W. H. ALLEN, *Receiver.*

To the COMMISSIONER *of the General Land Office.*

ALPHABETICAL LIST of cases reported on during the Session of 1828, *by the Register and Receiver at St. Augustine.*

No. of Report.	No. of Claim.		No. of Acres.
		A.	
1	8	Andrew, Robert - - - -	500
1	38	Anderson, George - - - -	450
2	3	Arnau, E. - - - -	100
2	24	Anderson, Robert, heirs - - -	100
2	28	Andrew, Robert - - - -	100
2	39	Andrew, Thomas - - - -	200
2	116	Atkinson, Andrew - - -	100
2	117	Andrews, Anth. heirs - - -	500
3	8	Acosta, Domingo S. - - -	8,000
3	9	Avice, Francis J. - - - -	500
3	10	Aguelar, Francisco - - -	30,000
3	11	Atkinson, George - - - -	15,000
3	12	Same - - - -	4,000
3	13	Arredondo, F. M. and Son - -	38,000
3	14	Same - - - -	50,000
3	15	Arredondo, J. M. - - -	40,000
3	16	Arredondo, F. M. - - -	250,000
3	18	Same - - - -	1,500
5	9	Ashton, John - - - -	640
5	31	Andrew, John - - - -	640
6	12	Avice, Francis J. - - - -	640
9	7 & 8	Alverez, Geronimo	
9	14	Arredondo, Jr. F. M.	
9	15	Alexander, J. heirs	
10	7	Anderson, George	
11	17	Arnau, Clara	
11	20	Andrew, John	
11	18	Arnau, Stephen	
15	8	Alverez, Antonio - - - -	1,500
15	16	Acosta, Margaret - - - -	341½ yds.
15	7	Atkinson, George - - - -	550
		B.	
1	1	Bunch, John - - - -	1,160
1	15 & 16	Brown and Clarke - - - -	400
1	48	Baya, Joseph, - - - -	130
1	50	Briggs, Cyrus - - - -	250
1	51	Same - - - -	100
1	73	Bunch, Elizabeth - - - -	100
2	86	Buyck and Dupont (Small Island)	
2	73	Bellamy, John - - - -	500
2	30	Barden, William - - - -	50

LIST—Continued.

No. of Report.	No. of Claim.		No. of Acres.
2	33	Broadaway, Delia - - - -	500
2	110	Backhouse, Thomas - - - -	500
2	109	Bethune, Farquhar - - - -	172
2	127	Burgo Peso, Pedro de - - -	20,000
2	4	Backhouse, Thomas - - - -	500
2	82	Buyck, Augustin - - - -	1,500
2	83	Same - - - - -	1,500
2	84	Same - - - - -	2,000
2	85	Same - - - - -	50,000
3	34	Burgevin, Andrew - - - -	500
3	35	Same - - - - -	500
5	4	Bellamy, Abraham - - - -	640
5	8	Burney, James - - - -	640
5	23	Bellamy, John - - - -	640
5	25	Same - - - - -	150
5	34	Bowden, Thomas - - - -	640
6	11	Ballard, Sarah - - - -	640
7	1	Brown, John F.	640
9	12	Bethune, Farquhar	
9	13	Bethune and Sibbald	
9	18 & 19	Bulow's, heirs	
10	12 & 14	Bruce, Joseph	
10	15	Bunnam, Joseph	
10	16	Beasme, George - - - -	
13	1	Beardon, Ab. and wife - - -	150
13	2	Brockington, Daniel - - - -	200
16	27	Besbord, Earl of - - - -	20,000
16	28	Berresford, John - - - -	20,000
16	28	Berresford, William - - - -	20,000
		C.	
1	26	Clarke, George J. F. - - - -	100
1	29	Christopher's, administrators - - -	500
1	33	Clarke, George - - - -	1,000
1	43	Cavedo, John - - - -	200
1	47	Chaires, Benjamin - - - -	300
1	74	Same - - - - -	300
1	76	Curtis, James - - - -	400
2	22	Cone, Joseph - - - - -	115
2	32	Collins, widow - - - -	1,200
2	45	Creighton, John - - - -	305
2	74	Cashen, Susan - - - -	300
2	76	Cain, William - - - -	200
2	77	Copeland, George - - - -	400
3	19	Copp, Belton A. - - - -	1,500

LIST—Continued.

No. of Report.	No. of Claim.		No. of Acres.
4	6	Carr, John - - - - -	250
4	8	Charles, Reuben - - - -	350
4	11	Crespo, Emanuel - - - -	640
6	1	Cooper, Adam - - - -	640
6	2	Caldez, M. J. - - - -	640
6	14	Caldez, J. - - - - -	640
9	2 & 45	Cashen's heirs	
10	2	Carnochan and Mitchell's assignees	
10	4	Campbell, Ann	
11	7	Capella, Lorenzo	
11	15 & 16	Cook, Margaret	
12	4	Clarke, George J. F. - - - -	4,000
12	8	Clarke, Charles M. - - - -	4,000
12	9 & 10	Clinch and McIntosh - - - -	2,000
12	14	Clarke, George J. F. - - -	350
12	20	Same - - - - -	2,000
12	30	Same - - - - -	1,000
12	16	Clarke, Charles and George - - -	1,000
12	17	Clarke, James - - - -	3,000
12	18	Clinch, Duncan - - - -	500
12	19	Clarke, Charles and George - - -	2,000
12	21	Clarke, Charles W. - - - -	375
12	22	Same - - - - -	300
12	23	Same - - - - -	1,576
12	26	Same - - - - -	2,300
12	27	Clarke, Daniel - - - -	500
12	28	Clarke, James - - - -	500
12	29	Clarke, Thomas - - - -	500
13	3	Christopher, Spicer - - - -	500
13	4	Carter, John M. - - - -	100
15	15	Crosby's heirs - - - -	2,000
16	2	Copp, Belton A. - - - -	1,000
16	26	Cooper, Sir William - - - -	20,000
16	34	Cassilis, The Earl - - - -	20,000
16	22	Carlisle, Jesse - - - -	640
12	1	Clarke, George, J. F. - - -	2,000
12	2	Same - - - - -	2,000
12	3	Same - - - - -	4,500
15	9	Clarke and Brown - - - -	3,000
		D.	
1	4	Dean, Patrick - - - -	995
1	6	Dill, Joseph - - - - -	500
1	52	Drummond, William - - - -	400
1	66	Dewees, Mary - - - -	500

LIST—Continued.

No. of Report.	No. of Claim.		No. of Acres
2	50	Demillier's heirs - - - -	170
2	52	Dell, James, - - - - -	500
2	55	Droiellard, Andrew - - - -	3,000
2	65	Dupont's heirs, 4 claims, (1850, 500, 500, & 1400.)	
2	66	Dell and McIntosh - - - -	500
2	78	Darley, James - - - -	500
2	79	Same - - - - -	500
2	80	Dupon, Paul - - - - -	3,000
2	113	Dry, William - - - -	1,000
2	114	Same } Lots St. Augustine.	
2	115	Same }	
2	121	Dupon, Paul - - - - -	3,000
3	1	Darley, James - - - -	23,000
3	2	Delesphine, Joseph - - - -	43,000
3	3	Same - - - - -	10,244
4	7	Dixon, John - - - - -	350
5	12	Durant, Francis - - - -	640
5	33	Daniel, William - - - -	640
5	37	Darling, James - - - -	640
10	32	Domingo, Dina	
11	8 & 11	Davis, Mary Ann	
13	5	Dewees' heirs - - - -	1,809½
13	6	Dexter, J. Horatio (Alachua)	
13	7	Dexter and Grace (3 miles square)	
13	8	Dexter, J. Horatio - - - -	2,000
13	9	Dorimas, Thomas P. - - - -	500
13	10	Drysdale and Rodman - - -	2,262
13	12	Darley, James - - - -	500
13	11	Delespine, Joseph - - - -	200
16	12	Dell, Maxey - - - -	700
		E.	
1	70	Ervin, James - - - -	125
2	120	Eubanks, Stephen - - - -	255
3	27	Eckford, Henry - - - -	46,080
4	5	Edge, John - - -	640
11	12	Estopa, Pedro	
13	13	Eubanks, Stephen - - - -	256
16	11	Same - - - - -	450
16	24	Evans, William - - - -	640
16	23	Elanier, Hardy - - - -	640
		F.	
1	7	Felany, F. - - - - -	1,200
1	10	Felany, James - - -	285

LIST—Continued.

No. of Report.	No. of Claim.		No. of Acres.
1	14	Faulk's heirs - - - -	100
1	54	Fitch's heirs - - - -	400
2	35	Fallis, A. - - - -	50
2	53	Faulk's heirs - - - -	250
2	67	Fish, Clarissa - - - -	150
2	124	Fontane, Pablo - - - -	3,000
9	6	Fallis, A.	
10	17	Fatio, Phillis	
11	2 & 4	Fusha, Francisca	
13	14	Frink, William - - - -	321
13	15	Frost, Isaac - - - -	1,500
13	16	Same - - - - -	2,000
13	17	Frazer, John, executor - - -	3,000
13	18	Fernandez, Domingo - - -	322
13	19	Fallis, E. (mill seat)	
15	1	Fatio, Francis J. and others - - -	750
15	13	Farraer, Francis, (Key Bacas)	
3	7	Fleming's heirs - - - -	20,000
5	14	Ford, Richard - - - -	640
3	37	Fitch, Thomas' heirs - - - -	4,500
3	38	Fernandez, Domingo - - - -	16,000
		G.	
1	49	Goodwin's heirs - - - -	640
1	72	Gibson, Edward R. - - - -	250
2	7	Gonzalez, John - - - -	1,000
2	18	Gibson, Edward R. - - - -	125
2	20	Gobert, Charlotte - - - -	100
2	49	Gould, Elias B. - - - -	500
2	68	Goodwin's heirs (3 cases)	
2	96	Gaudry, B. John - - - -	3,000
2	129	Gobert, Charles - - - -	2,000
3	4	Gomez, E. M. - - - -	12,000
3	20	Gay, A. - - - -	500
4	3	Garcia's heirs, John - - - -	200
5	19	Gilbert, Robert - - - -	232
5	27	Gardner, William - -	640
6	4	Gonzalez, Andrew - - - -	640
6	5	Gomez, Antonio - - -	640
6	6	George, Julian - - - -	640
6	9	Godoya, J. M. - - -	640
9	21	Gould, Elias B	
10	5	Gui, Francis	
10	41	Gill, Viccute	
12	5	Gould, E. B. - - - -	500

LIST—Continued.

No. of Report.	No. of Claim.		No. of Acres.
12	12	Garvin, William - - - -	3,000
13	20	Gilbert, Robert - - - -	200
13	21	Same - - - - -	300
13	22	Gennings, John - - - -	250
15	12	Gaudry, B. John - - - -	1,500
16	19	Guibert, Lewis - - - -	640
16	25	Grosvenor, the Earl - - -	12,000
2	131	Garcia, Sebastian } (Lots outside of the gate.)	
2	132	Same }	
		H.	
1	36	Hurlbert, Daniel - - - -	300
1	2	Harrold, Moses - - - -	395
1	3	Huertas, Antonio - - - -	800
1	11	Hollingsworth, William - - -	150
1	28	Hurlbert, Daniel - - - -	200
1	53	Hagin's heirs - - - -	200
1	60	Hall, James - - - -	450
1	61	Same - - - - -	250
1	62	Hudnall's heirs - - - -	100
1	63	Hernandez, Martin - - - -	2,000
2	6	Houston, John - - - -	700
2	10	Hall, W. F. - - - -	2,000
2	21	Hurlbert, D. - - - -	125
2	23	Hutchinson, R. - - - -	450
2	29	Hart, D. C. - - - -	150
2	38	Hudnall's heirs - - - -	900
2	42	Hart, William - - - -	1,400
2	48	Hall, Nathaniel's heirs - - -	400
2	54	Hartley, F. - - - -	400
2	56	Hull, William - - - -	500
2	62	Hibberson and Yonge - - -	2,000
2	72	Same - - - - -	2,000
2	98	Same - - - - -	45
2	99	Hutchinson, Robert - - - -	150
3	22	Hernandez, J. M. - - - -	10,000
3	23	Same - - - - -	5,000
3	24	Same - - - - -	5,000
4	2	Hogins, Eleanor - - - -	640
5	5	Haddock, William - - - -	640
5	7	Hart, William - - - -	640
5	36	Haddock, Z.'s heirs - - - -	640
6	15	Hagins, D. - - - -	640
6	16	Hall, John - - - -	640
10	9 & 11	Hernandez, Jos. M.	
10	10	Hernandez, Martin	

LIST—Continued.

No. of Report.	No. of Claim.		No. of Acres.
10	42	Hudson, Ab.	
11	1	Hernandez, Jose	
13	23	Hollingsworth, Wm. - - - -	250
13	24	Hayden, Mary - - - -	250
13	25	Hendricks, Isaac - - - -	450
15	14	Hernandez, Jos. M. - - -	3,200
16	32	Hastings, Marquis of - - - -	20,000
16	37	Hughes, Jane - - - -	2,000
16	10	Hovey, Charles - - - -	400
16	7	Hartley, Frederick - - - -	400
16	9	Higginbotham, Thomas - - -	200
2	130	Hernandez, Joseph M. (undefined.)	
		J.	
1	31	Jones, John - - - - - -	100
2	118	Same - - - - -	500
5	1	Same - - - - -	640
5	6	Jones, Thomas - - - -	640
10	8	Isaac, Robert	
14	1	Jones, William Thomas - - -	2,000
		K.	
2	75	Kehr, John - - - - - -	300
2	100	King, Samuel - - - -	300
3	33	King, Ralph - - - - - -	5,000
8	11 to 13	Kinlock, Fr. (2,350, 500, and 500.)	500
9	3	Kehr, J. D.	
		L.	
1	5	Leonardy, R. - - - -	1,400
1	34	Lang's heirs - - - -	200
1	36	Ledwith, Michael - - - -	250
1	37	Ledwith, Garret - - - -	100
1	39	Lopez, Bartholomew & Co. - - -	17
1	59	Lamb's heirs - - - -	200
1	77	Long, George's heirs - - - -	600
2	5	Levy, Moses - - - -	500
2	11	Lesla, Flora - - - -	500
2	31	Lewis, James, jr. - - - -	50
2	36	Lynch, Michael - - - -	335
2	61	Ladd, William - - - -	1,525
2	69	Love, John - - - -	300
5	35	Long, Joseph and Matthew - - -	640
11	6	Lorenzo, John, widow of	

LIST—Continued.

No. of Report.	No. of Claim.		No. of Acres.
11	19	Lopez, Bartholomew	
13	26	Lane, William	300
13	27	Same	300
13	28	Same	100
13	29	Same	400
13	30	Long, George	300
13	31	Long's heirs, George	350
		M.	
1	35	Miranda, Peter	790
1	42	Mestre, John	50
1	44	McIntosh, John	800
1	55	McGirt, James	300
1	56	Same	300
1	57	Same	80
1	58	Medicis, Francis	400
1	65	Murat, Achilles	1,200
2	8	McDonnell, V. D.	800
2	9	Mitchell, P.	2,000
2	19	Morrison, George	150
2	40	Martin, H. B.	400
2	41	Murphey, Thomas	3,000
2	57	Mills, Joseph	200
2	60	McCormick, P.	2,000
2	14	McIntosh, John H.	2,000
2	81	Monroe, James	2,000
2	87 to 94	McGirt's	
2	97	Mitchell, Peter	550
2	101	Martenis, A. widow of	70
3	17	Miranda, Peter	640
3	21	Same	2,000
5	30	Mott, Emanuel D.	640
6	3	Michaco, Antonio	640
4	12	Miller, Robert	200
9	9	Mills, Maria	
9	20	Mitchell, Robert	
10	1	Mitchell, Robert	
10	3	Moliner, A.	
10	6	Mitchell, Peter	
10	18	Moore, Jacob	
10	19	Mariano, John	
10	20	Moore, John	
10	21	Moore, Patrico	
10	22	McQueen, Harry	
10	23	Mariano, Clara	

LIST—Continued.

No. of Report.	No. of Claim.		No. of Acres.
12	15	McDowell & Black - - - -	450
13	32	McClure, John M. - - - -	900
13	33	Marshall, Manuel - - - -	250
13	34	McQueen's, John, heirs - - -	10,000
13	35	Mill's, William, heirs - - -	5,000
13	36	Meers, John - - - -	200
13	37	Munroe, William - - - -	300
13	38	Morrison's, George, heirs, undefined	
14	2	McIntosh, John H. - - - -	3,274
16	1	McDowell & Black - - - -	1,000
16	16	Mitchell, Peter - - - -	3,500
16	17	Miller, Robert, undefined	
16	4	Miller, Robert and wife, Martin's island	
		N.	
2	15	Nobles, Hannah - - - -	1,000
5	15	Nicholas, Peter - - - -	640
11	9	Noda, Joseph	
11	13	Same	
12	7	Napier, Thomas - - - -	1,000
12	13	Same - - - -	1,000
12	11	Same - - - -	1,000
		O.	
1	13	O'Neal's heirs - - - -	300
1	19	O'Neal M. - - - -	243
3	5	O'Hara, Daniel - - - -	15,000
3	31	Ortega, Anne - - - -	100
3	32	Same - - - -	100
		P.	
1	12	Pritchard's heirs - - - -	250
1	20	Pilot, James - - - -	622
1	21	Pritchard, Eleanor - - - -	270
1	41	Palliser, Francis - - - -	2,000
1	71	Pafry, Andrew - - - -	126
2	44	Pike's heirs - - - -	400
2	51	Paz, Francisco - - - -	1,500
2	63	Pilot, James - - - -	496
2	64	Same - - - -	356
2	102	Pritchard's heirs - - - -	700
4	1	Pacety, Andrew - - - -	640
5	20	Prevat, Joseph R. - - - -	640

LIST—Continued.

No. of Report.	No. of Claim.		No. of Acres.
5	24	Prevat, Thomas - - - -	640
6	7	Pomfron, P. - - - -	640
6	8	Pancier, Antonio - - - -	640
11	10	Parety, Andrew	
13	39	Plummer, James - - - -	265
13	40	Plummer, Daniel - - - -	600
16	20	Picket, Seymour - - - -	640
16	39	Patterson, James - - - -	250
		R.	
1	9	Richard, J. B. - - - -	230
1	18	Rose, James - - - -	25
1	24	Richard, Francis - - - -	650
1	36	Roderiguez, S. - - - -	2,[illegible]00
1	40	Richard, Francis - - - -	1,025
2	12	Rowlins, Susan - - - -	200
2	43	Rayes, Joseph B. - - - -	1,700
2	37	Rushing, John G. - - - -	80
5	29	Rawlins, Benjamin - - - -	640
7	2	Rowse, James - - - -	640
7	3	Rawls, Cotton - - - -	640
9	10	Roderiguez, D.	
10	31	Rose, James	
10	33	Ribas, Bob	
10	34	Richo, Joe	
11	05	Rogero, Antonia	
13	41	Rivas, Isaac's heirs - - - -	4,000
13	42	Richard, James' heirs - - -	200
13	43	Russell, Samuel - - - -	300
15	6	Roderiguez, Nicholas - - -	300
16	31	Rolle, Lord John - - - -	20,000
16	49	Rattenburg, Freeman J. - - -	2,600
16	50	Same - - - -	50,000
		S.	
1	23	Sabate, Pablo Casicola	
1	25	Sasportas, J. - - - -	425
1	30	Solana, Philip - - - -	30
1	32	Scipio, a negro - - - -	25
1	45	Segui, John - - - -	107
1	64	Sauchez, Francis P. - - - -	2,000
1	67	Sauchez, Joseph M. - - - -	200
1	68	Smith, Hannah - - - -	$389\frac{2}{3}$
1	69	Smith, Josiah - - - -	1,000

LIST—Continued.

No. of report.	No. of claim.		No. of Acres.
1	75	Smith, Josiah - - - -	400
2	1	Suazez, B. - - - -	50
2	2	Sabaste, Pablo - - - -	2,500
2	16	Suarez, Antonio, administrator - -	500
2	26	Starkey, Josiah - - - -	455
2	71	Sauchez, Francis P. - - - -	2,000
2	111	Saunders, William H. G. - - -	1,200
2	128	Smith, Hannah - - - -	400
3	25	Sauchez, Frs. P. - - - -	1,400
3	26	Same - - - -	500
3	29	Segui, Dina, - - - -	5,333
3	30	Same - - - -	4,000
4	4	Silcox, William - - - -	640
4	9	Solana, Bartho, - - - -	640
4	10	Solana, Margareta - - - -	640
5	2	Strong, John B. - - - -	640
5	3	Swenney, Henry - - - -	640
5	10	Solana, Manuel - - - -	640
5	22	Stallings, Ann - - - -	640
5	28	Stephens, N. - - - -	640
6	13	Stanly, S. - - - -	640
6	17	Silcox, John - - - -	640
7	4	Silcox, Wade - - - -	640
9	1	Segui, Bernard	
9	11	Scott, Maria R.	
9	16	Smith, Josiah, heirs	
10	24	Segui, Benjamin	
10	25	Sauchez, Joseph	
10	26	Savelly, Maria	
10	27	Sauchez, Susan	
10	30	Sanco, Mingo	
10	44	Sauchez, Jos. S.	
"	45	Same	
"	46	Same	
"	47	Same	
"	48	Same	
"	49	Same	
11	3	Solana, Philip	
12	6	Simonton - - - - -	1,500
12	25	Stores - - - - - -	500
13	44	Suydam, James - - - -	500
13	45	Suarez, Anthony - - - -	500
13	46	Solana, Philip - - - - -	100
15	2	Sauchez, Francis P. - - - -	800
15	3	Segui, Benardo - - - -	7,000
15	11	Sauchez, Francis P. - - - -	100

LIST—Continued.

No. of report.	No. of claim.		No. of Acres.
16	3	Sauchez, Francis P.	1,000
16	13	Same	500
16	14	Sauchez, Jos. S.	400
16	15	Sauchez, John	400
16	18	Summerrall, Joseph	150
16	21	Scurry, David	640
		T.	
1	22	Terran, Francisco D.	300
1	27	Triay, Antonio	1,500
2	70	Tillet, George	250
2	95	Tate, Sarah	450
2	59	Turner, David	90
2	104	Tool, James	945
2	105	Triay, Francis	
2	106	Travers, William	100
2	107	Tucker, Isaac	200
2	108	Triay, G. Key Bacas	
2	112	Travers, Wm. Agent Yellowly	500
2	119	Tucker, Ezekiel	150
2	126	Tucker, H.	100
5	11	Toy, John	640
5	16	Tanner, Nathaniel	640
5	21	Tice, Richard	640
8	1	Travers, Agent, Forbes	500
8	2	Same	500
8	3	Same	500
8	4	Same	500
8	5	Same	500
8	6	Same	750
8	7	Same, Agent, Panton	500
8	8	Same	500
8	9	Same	500
8	10	Same	2,000
10	28	Travers, Terry	
10	29	Travers, Tony	
11	14	Triay, Francis	
13	47	Thomas, William	200
13	48	Taylor, George, heirs, Casicola	
13	49	Same, San Pablo	
13	50	Same	64
13	51	Same, saw mill	
13	52	Tillet, George, undefined	
15	10	Travers, William	450
16	30	Templeton, Lord	20,000

LIST—Continued.

No. of report.	No. of claim.		No. of Acres.
16	35	Tonyn, George, heirs - - - -	20,000
16	36	Same - - - - -	125
		U.	
2	58	Ulmer, William - - - -	200
13	53	Uptigrove, John - - - -	100
		V.	
2	122	Villalonga, Miguel - - - -	16
2	123		
2	103	Vass, Gachalar - - - - -	250
10	13	Villalonga, Margaret	
10	35	Valentine, Lucia	
		W.	
1	17	Whitmore's heirs - - - -	150
2	13	Wiggins, Isabella - - - -	300
2	25	Same - - - - -	300
2	27	White, Jos. F. - - - -	250
2	34	Williams, a negro - - - -	300
2	46	Webber, George - - - -	100
2	17	Williams, A. heirs - - - -	150
2	125	Worldly, Jacob, undefined	
3	28	Ward, Jasper - - - - -	128,000
3	36	Wordly, Jacob, 4 miles square	
5	13	Watson, Jos. - - - - -	640
5	17	Wilson, Jesse - - - - -	640
5	18	Williamson, Blake - - - -	640
5	26	Williamson, Wm. - - - -	640
5	32	Williamson, David - - - -	640
9	17	White, Jos. F.	
13	54	Woodlar, James - - - -	200
13	55	Williamson, John - - - -	850
13	56	Walker, Robert	
15	4	Williams, heirs - - - -	2,020
15	5	Same - - - -	180
16	5	Wiles, A. - - - - -	184
16	6	Woods, James - - - - -	75
10	36	Wiggins, Ann	
10	37	Wiggins, Isabella	
10	38 & 39	Wiggins, Nancy	
12	24	Weightman, Richard - - -	200
16	8	Woods, Theo. T. - - - -	370

LIST--Continued.

No. of report.	No. of claim.		No. of Acres.
16	33	Waterford, Marquis of - - - - -	20,000
10	40	Wright, John	
10	43	Waterman's heirs	
13	57	White, Jos. F. - - - - - -	200
		Y.	
2	47	Yonge, Thomas - - - -	1,100
3	6	Yonge, Philip R. - - - -	25,000
6	10	Yelvington, Jacob - - - -	640
16	40	Yates, David, heirs - - - -	100
16	41	Same - - - -	158
16	42	Same - - - -	100
16	43	Same - - - -	640
16	44	Same - - - -	500
16	45	Same - - - -	336
16	46	Yates - - - - - -	625
16	47	Yates, a town lot, No. 2	
16	48	Yates, do No. 3	

REPORT No. I.

No. 1.

JOHN BUNCH, *Claimant—for 1168 acres of land.*

On the petition of John Bunch, 2160 acres of land were granted by Gov. White in 1804, at Oak Forest in Mosquitoe. On the survey of Robert McHardy, it was found that there were at that place 1168 acres only. Bunch cultivated the land for several years, and in the year 1819, Governor Coppinger gave to him a royal title for this last quantity. By the rule adopted by this Board, that, on a previous concession, a royal title, signed by the Spanish Governor, though dated subsequently to the 24th February 1818, should be considered as full evidence of the performance of all conditions made necessary by the ordinance of the King, 1790, under which the land was granted, this claim is confirmed. Thomas H. Dummett is the present claimant by purchase from Bunch.

No. 2.

MOSES HARROLD, *Claimant—for 395 acres of land.*

Moses Harrold petitioned the Government for lands, for head rights, and there were granted to him on the 21st April, 1807, 395 acres of land, on the river Nassau; which land was surveyed by John Purcell on the 30th November of the same year, and on the 8th May, 1821, Governor Coppinger issued a royal title in favor of said Harrold, for the said land. It is therefore confirmed.

No. 3.

ANTONIO HUERTES, *Claimant—for 800 acres of land.*

Antonio Huertes petitioned the Government for the lands under the royal order of 1790, and on the 20th October, 1813, Governor Kendelan issued to him a royal title for 800 acres on the West side of the river St. Sebastian, nearly opposite the city of St. Augustine. The title against the United States is good.

No. 4.

PATRICK DEAN, *Claimant—for 995 acres of land.*

Patrick Dean petitioned the Government for lands under the royal order of 1790, and there were granted to him, by decree of the 31st August, 1804, 995 acres, situated in the Territory of Mosquitoe, on the West side of the river Halifax, opposite Pelican Island; and on the 4th June, 1819, Governor Coppinger issued to the heirs of said Dean, a royal title for said lands. This claim is confirmed for reasons in No. 1.

No. 5.

ROQUE LEORNADY, *Claimant—for* 1400 *acres of land.*

Roque Leornady petitioned the Government on the 3d January, 1792, for lands under the royal order of 1790, situated on the Pablo road, about 15 miles from St. Augustine, on the North river, and Governor Quesada allows him to settle on the land. Andrew Burgevin surveyed said land on the 28th April, 1819, for the heirs of said Leornady, who apply to Governor Coppinger for a royal title for the same, which is complied with on the 25th May, 1821, for 1400 acres in the same place. This claim is confirmed. A concession in 1792 and the royal title in 1821, though the last is not of itself good, according to the provisions of the treaty, it is good evidence of the performance of the conditions inherent in the grant.

No. 6.

JOSEPH DILL, *Claimant—for* 500 *acres of land.*

Joseph Dill petitioned the Government for lands under the royal order of 1790; and on the 3d January, 1803, 500 acres were granted him on the South side of St. John's river, at a place called Mill Creek, 40 miles from the city. Robert Clarke Maxey purchased said land from Dill, and on the 18th May, 1821, Governor Coppinger issued to the heirs of said Maxey a royal title for said land. It is therefore confirmed.

No. 7.

FERNANDO FELANY, *Claimant—for* 1200 *acres of land.*

Fernando Felany petitioned the Government for lands under the royal order of 1790, and on the 20th December, 1792, there were granted to him 1200 acres, at a place called Tufily, about two leagues South of St. Augustine; on the 18th May, 1819, Governor Coppinger issues in his favor a royal title. It is therefore confirmed.

No. 8.

ROBERT ANDREW, *Claimant—for* 500 *acres of land.*

In 1793, Don Pedro Marrot surveyed to Robert Andrew 500 acres of land, at a place called San Roberts, and Governor White issued to him a royal title, on the 6th April, 1809. The title is good. Benjamin Chaires is the present claimant.

No. 9.

JOHN B. RICHARD, *Claimant—for* 230 *acres of land.*

In 1803, John B. Richard obtained a grant or concession for the land claimed. It is in proof before the Board, that Richard lived on, and cultivated the land until 1810, at which time he died. His widow then moved off of the land, but, as it appears, did not remain away long enough to forfeit her claim, but returned in a short time and perfected it. It is therefore confirmed.

No. 10.

James Felany, *Claimant—for 285 acres of land.*

James Felany petitioned the Government on the 17th November, 1815, for the lands formerly abandoned by Boeson, situated on the river Matanzas, and on the same day, month, and year, Governor Estrada grants him 185 acres of land, being the quantity he is entitled to for his head rights, according to the number of his family. Felany also presents to the Board a certificate of Pierra, in which he states that Governor White granted to Pedro Chuet one hundred acres of land adjoining the above tract, on the 3d September, 1805, which was purchased by Felany by deed attached to the certificate of concession. On the 10th of April, 1821, Felany applies to the Government for permission to have the lands above mentioned surveyed, which is granted by Governor Coppinger; and on the 6th October, 1821, Andrew Burgevin surveys for said Felany 285 acres of land in the place pointed out.

The permission and order of the Governor to survey the lands, as then the property and in possession of the claimant, we have considered evidence of continued possession in him up to 1821, about which time the government passed away from the Spaniards. It is therefore confirmed.

No. 11.

William Hollingsworth, *Claimant—for 150 acres of land.*

In 1792, Governor Quesada, granted to William Valentine 150 acres of land on the river St. John, and directed Marrot to survey it. The survey was made by Marrot, and proof has been adduced that Valentine, or Hollingsworth, to whom he sold it, and who is the present claimant, have been in actual and continued possession of the land up to this time. It is therefore confirmed.

No. 12.

The heirs of Robert Pritchard, *Claimants—for 250 acres of land.*

In 1791, Marrot, who had been directed by Quesada, the Governor, to survey lands to the settlers in the country who might want them, and the quantity to which, by, the regulations they were entitled, certifies that he had surveyed this land to Thomas Bowden. Two witnesses have deposed that Bowden was for many years in possession of the land. It is therefore confirmed.

No. 13.

The heirs of W. O'Neal, *Claimants—for 300 acres of land.*

Here is a Royal title, dated the 15th June, 1810. The title declares that the grant was made under the Royal order of 1790. It is therefore confirmed.

No. 14.

The heirs of Sarah Foulks, *Claimants—for* 100 *acres of land.*

Don Pedro Marrot, commissioner appointed to distribute lands, according to the orders of His Majesty, had surveyed for Margaret Jones three caballeras (100 acres of land) situated at a place called Sheron, on the East side of St. John's River, on the 20th February, 1793. The land was purchased of —— Jones, by the ancestor of the present claimant, and witness certifies that the parties have been possessed of the tract claimed for many years. It is therefore confirmed.

Nos. 15 and 16.

G. S. Brown and S. Clarke, *Claimants—for* 400 *acres of land.*

Edward Wanton petitions the Government, on the 11th November, 1801, for the following tracts of land for head rights, to wit: One hundred acres situated between Picolata and the plantation of Manuel Solana, on the river St. Johns, and six hundred and fifty acres on Cedar Hammoc, about two miles and a half to the South of Solana's, on said river St. Johns, in front of Tocoi Creek; and on the 23d November, 1801, Governor White makes the following decree: "Let there be granted to this party the land which he solicits without injury to a third person, and until, according to the persons he may have for its cultivation, there shall be measured to him the corresponding quantity;" and Governor Coppinger, on the 26th April, 1820, issued to him a Royal title. These two claims are therefore confirmed. Clarke and Brown claim title by purchase from Wanton.

No. 17.

The heirs of Robert Whitmore, *Claimants—for* 150 *acres of land.*

This tract is claimed by and has been confirmed to William Hollingsworth, No. 11 of this abstract.

No. 18.

James Rose, *Claimant—for* 25 *acres of land.*

The title produced in this case, is a certificate of Thomas D. Aguilar, that Governor White granted to James Rose, a free man (black) 25 acres of land in Pibot's Swamp. The negro applied for 100, but the Governor granted no more than 25; two witnesses have been brought forward to prove cultivation and continued possession by the claimant. It is therefore confirmed.

No. 19.

MARGARETTA O'NEAL, *Claimant—for 243 acres of land.*

Don Pedro Marrot, Commissioner for the distribution of lands by order of His Majesty, had surveyed for Margaretta O'Neal, two tracts of land, as follows: One tract containing 9 cavalleras and 7 acres, or 307 acres on Lansford Creek, at a place called New Hope, on 16th April, 1792. The other tract, containing 7 cavalleras and 10 acres, or 243 acres, on Lansford Creek, at a place called O'Neal, made 17th April, 1792. And on the 13th March, 1807, Governor White issued a royal title, in favor of M. O'Neal, for the last mentioned tract of 243 acres, under the royal order of 29th October, 1790. This last is therefore confirmed.

No. 20.

JAMES PELOT, *Claimant—for 620 acres of land.*

It appears that the present claimant has presented to this Board three claims, which should be reduced to the last number of 620 acres, which was evidently given as a substitution of the others. James Pelot has no evidence of his claim but the certificate of Marrot, dated in 1793, without any accompanying evidence of cultivation. John Francis Pelot has a certificate of Pierra in 1803, that the land on Amelia Island was granted by Governor White. It appears by many circumstances, that the claimants are one and the same persons, in the survey called James, and in the grant called John Francis. In support of this position, the witness Farquhar Bethune, who proves a long continued cultivation of the land on Amelia Island, calls the claimant there James Pilot. Geo. Clarke surveyed the land. Suffice it to say, that if the land on Amelia Island was or was not given in lieu of that on St. John's, and if the claimants, James and John Francis Pelot, were, or were not the same person, no more can be confirmed that 620 acres. James Pelot has produced no evidence to his claims on the river, and they must be rejected. John Francis has proved, that the land on Amelia was cultivated for many years, and although he is called James by the affiant Bethune, yet there can be no mistake in the land itself. It lies on Amelia Island: 640 were granted by White; 620 surveyed by Clarke; and it is confirmed to Pelot by whatever name he be called, James or John Francisco.

No. 21.

ELEANOR PRITCHARD, *Claimant—for 270 acres of land.*

In 1808 sundry witnesses being produced by Eleanor Pritchard, the widow of Robert Pritchard, to prove to Governor White, the number of her family, black and white. Don John Percell was ordered to survey to the claimant "two hundred and seventy acres of land, which correspond to the interested, her children and slaves," in the place which the certificate points out on the river St. John's. Jos. Somerall and Joseph Hagen, two witnesses introduced by the claimant, have proved the continued possession and cultivation of the place claimed by the then widow, now the wife of James Hall, up to the date of their deposition, the 15th June, 1824. It is confirmed.

No. 22.

FRANCISCO DIAZ TERRAN, *Claimant—for 300 acres of land.*

Fr. Diaz Terran petitioned the Government, on the 9th March, 1797, for 300 acres of land, situated on the South point of Amelia Island, under the royal order of 1790. The Governor passed the memorial to the Commandant of Engineers, for his report, who reported in favor of allowing Terran to settle on the lands petitioned for, but that, "should the Government be obliged to order the inhabitants to retire from Amelia to St. John's river, then he was of opinion, that the memorialist should not be permitted to claim damages;" to which Governor White makes the following, decree on the 11th of the same month and year: "Let there be granted to the petitioner the land which he solicits, without injury to a third person, according to the number of his family, and precise conditions of conforming to what is set forth in the foregoing report, relative to his not claiming satisfaction for injuries, in case that, for the better service of the King, they be ordered to leave the lands set forth, and that the inhabitants thereof retire on the River St. Johns." The depositions of two witnesses, taken in the State of Georgia, are filed in this claim, to show occupancy of this land by the grantee." They are sufficient to prove the fact of possession, but not the length of its continuance. This may have been an omission of the Justice before whom they were taken. It is too late now to remedy the defect, and we have deemed it better to confirm this claim, than to do probable injustice by rejecting it.

No. 23.

PABLO SABATE, *Claimant—for ——— acres of land.*

"I certify that, on examination of the Office of the Public Archives, I find no grants of the above land from the Government; but, as early as the 23d July, 1760, there is a sale on record from John Elegio de la Puente to Jesse Fish, and on the 31st March, 1792, the said land was sold by a decision of the judicial tribunal of this then Province, as the property of Fish, and purchased by John Taton, and afterwards sold to intermediate purchasers until the 7th September, 1809, when Susan Madin, widow of Brian Conner, sold the same to Pablo Sabate, the present claimant." This seems to be a grant in which case the original is lost. The judicial recognition of its validity by the Spanish Government, as appears by the above certificate of F. J. Fatio, and the sanction of the sale to Taton, is sufficient to ground a decree of confirmation.

No. 24.

FRANCIS RICHARD, *Claimant—for 650 acres of land.*

Governor Quesada granted this land to one Samuel Russell, in 1795. Russell lived on the land, as is proved to the Board, more than ten years, and sold to Richard. In 1821, by order of the Government, it was surveyed to the claimant, to whom it is now confirmed.

No. 25.

ISAAC SASPORTAS, *Claimant—for* 425 *acres of land.*

This is the same claim which was rejected by the Board in the session of 1827, as dated after the 24th January, 1818, and is so reported to Congress on abstract No. 2. It appears now, that the royal title then produced to the Board, dated 6th May, 1818, was granted on a previous concession, issued on the 10th June, 1817. On the production of this new evidence of title, the Commissioners have no hesitation in deciding that the claim is a good one, and should be confirmed.

No. 26.

GEORGE CLARK, *Claimant—for* 100 *acres of land.*

John Cabedo petitioned the Government, on 23d February, 1801, for permission to transfer his right to George Clark, of one hundred acres of land, situated on Guana Creek, to which Governor White made the following decree on the 25th February, 1801: "The transfer is permitted which J. Cabedo makes in favor of George Clark, of the 100 acres he obtained on Guana Creek, in consequence of which there shall be given to Clark the corresponding document for his security, returning to Miguel Acosta the certificate accompanying this memorial, with the note attached to the same." This sale from Cabedo to Clark, when sanctioned by Gov. White, is good proof of conditions performed. It is therefore confirmed.

No. 27.

ANTONIO FRIAY, *Claimant—for* 1500 *acres of land.*

Antonio Friay petitioned the Government, and there were granted to him on the 23d September, 1811, fifteen hundred acres of land, situated on the east side of the River St Johns, opposite the mouth of the River Okelewaja, and on the 21st February, 1821, said Friay petitioned the Government to issue to him a royal title for said land, which was done by Governor Coppinger on the 9th same month and year. In this case the concession is dated in 1811, the royal title in 1821. The concession is always conditional, and the royal title, though after the 24th January, 1818, is good proof of the performance of those conditions. It is confirmed.

No. 28.

DANIEL HURLBERT, *Claimant—for* 200 *acres of land.*

On the 22d August, 1814, a public sale took place in the city of Augustine, by order of the Government, of 200 acres of land, situated 5 miles north of the said city, the property of Jose Antonio de Yguiniz, which land was purchased by D. Hurlbert, and on the 26th same month and year, acknowledged by the Tribunal to be the property of said Hurlbert. This is somewhat similar to the claim of Pablo Sabate, No 23 of this abstract, a sale of land to which no original grant is found, ordered and recognized by the Judicial Tribunal of the country. It is confirmed.

No. 29.

William G. Christopher's *adm. Claimant—for* 500 *acres of land.*

Don Pedro Marrot, Commissioner for the distribution of lands in East Florida, had surveyed for Spicer Christopher, on the 15th February, 1792, 15 caballerias or 500 acres of land, situated on the River Nassau, at a place called Santa Maria, and on the 8th April, 1809, Governor White issued to said Christopher a royal title for said land. It is confirmed.

No. 30.

Philip Solana, *Claimant—for* 30 *acres of land.*

Thomas Aguilar, Secretary of Government, certifies that, to a memorial presented by Pedro de Cala, dated 3d March, 1807, praying for 61 acres of those formerly granted to Antonio Martinez, situated at a place called Muchie, Governor White made the following decree on the 10th March of the same year: "Let there be granted to the interested, 30 acres of land of the 140 which are granted to Antonio Martinez with the condition, that he must cultivate the land without intermission, and should he not comply, he will be deprived of the same, and in future no land whatever shall be granted him. Being obliged at the same time to deliver in the Secretary's office the certificate which was delivered to him from said office on the 4th April, 1804, for 20 acres, which were granted him on a small island to the south of the Matanzas." The grantee afterwards sold to P. Solana, the present claimant, with the consent of the Government, on the 30th June, 1821. This sale in 1821, with the consent of the Government, we consider conclusive to show the performance of all precedent conditions, express or implied. Confirmed.

No. 31.

John Jones, *Claimant—for* 100 *acres of land.*

This land was conceded to John Jones on the 26th August, 1803, who cultivated and possessed it, as Joseph Hagen has testified, for more than 25 years. It is situated on the west side of Trout Creek, and on the north of St. John's River. It is confirmed.

No. 32.

Scipio, *(a free Negro) Claimant—for* 25 *acres of land.*

Scipio, a free Black, petitioned the Government, on the 12th September, 1809, for 100 acres of land, situated on St. John's River, at a place called Padanaram, bounded on the N. W. by the lands of Dr. Travers, and on the S. E. by Six Mile Creek, to which Gov. White made the following decree, on the 9th October, 1809: "Let there be granted to the petitioner only 25 acres of land, in the place which he solicits, without injury to a third person, and shall cultivate the same without intermission." It is in evidence before the Board that Scipio cultivated the land for the requisite number of years. It is therefore confirmed to him.

No. 33.

George J. F. Clarke, *Claimant—for* 1000 *acres of land.*

This claim is supported by a concession in 1817, and a royal title in the month of August, 1818. It was not strictly regular, that a royal title should be issued until ten years had elapsed after the date of the concession and occupancy proved by the Claimant. The Governor, in this case, as in many others, has departed from the strict rules; nevertheless, the claim must be confirmed.

No. 34.

The Heirs of Isaac Lang, *Claimants—for* 200 *acres of land.*

Don Pedro Marrot, commissioned Judge by His Excellency the Commander in Chief of this Province of East Florida, for the survey of lands, ordered to be distributed, by command of His Majesty, certifies, on the 4th March, 1792, he had surveyed, by Samuel Eastlake, surveyor for Isaac Lang, six caballerias, or 200 acres of land, situated on Little St. Mary's River. It appears by reference to Marrot's list of persons to whom land had been surveyed, that this person is one of them, and he has produced a witness who proves cultivation four or five years. This perhaps is as much as should be required after so long a lapse of time. The claim is confirmed.

No. 35.

Peter Miranda, *Claimant—for* 790 *acres of land.*

Pedro Miranda petitioned the Government for Lands, under the Royal order of 1815, and on the 17th July, 1816, Governor Coppinger issued to said Miranda a Royal title for 790 acres, situated on the River Matanzas, to the South of St. Augustine. Charles Robio filed the claim. Confirmed.

No. 36.

Santo Rodriguez, *Claimant—for* 2000 *acres of land.*

Santo Rodriguez petitioned the Government, on the 22d December, 1817, for 2000 acres of land, under the Royal order of 1815, situated on the East side of St. John's River, on Dunn's Lake, to which Gov. Coppinger makes the following decree on the 24th January, 1818; "Let there be granted to the petitioner, the 2000 acres of land, in the place which he solicits, without injury to a third person, for which there shall be issued to him the Title in fee simple from Notary's office of Government and Royal Domain." George Clark surveyed the above tract on the 6th April, 1818. Confirmed.

No. 36.

MICHAEL LEDWITH, *Claimant—for* 250 *acres of land.*

Concession in 1804, on the River Nassau, on Lafton's Creek, proof by two witnesses that he cultivated it many years, and that it has never been out of the possession of Ledwith, the grantee, and his representatives. Cyrus Briggs claims for himself and others, the lawful heirs of Ledwith. It is confirmed.

No. 37.

GARRET LEDWITH, *Claimant—for Pelot's Island, about* 100 *acres of land.*

A concession by Governor White, in June, 1803, for Pelot's Island, about 100 acres, proof of possession by two witnesses, until the latter part of 1813. Cyrus Briggs claims for himself and others, the lawful heirs of Ledwith. It is confirmed.

No. 38.

GEORGE ANDERSON, *Claimant—for* 450 *acres of land.*

This land is situated in the Territory of Mosquitoe, "on the North by John Addison, on the South by the River Tomoka." Claimant holds by a deed made to Mr. Kerr, (from whom he inherits) by Gabriel W. Perpall the grantee. Perpall obtained a Royal title to the Land from Kindelan, under the order of 1790, in 1815. It is confirmed.

No. 39.

JUAN JOANEDA, BARTHOLOME LOPEZ, AND BARTHOLOME LEUFRIO, *Claimants*—17 *acres of land.*

Juan Joaneda, Bartholome Lopez, and Bartholome Leufrio, obtained from the British Government, 17 acres of land, situated between Bridge Creek and the River St. Sebastian, in the city of St. Augustine, and in the cession of this then province to the crown of Spain, it was confirmed to them by Governor Zespedez, and lastly by Governor White, who not only confirmed what his predecessor had done, but gave them permission to alienate the same. Of this, Gould claims one acre. The whole claim is good, and we confirm it.

No. 40.

FRANCIS RICHARD, *Claimant*—1025 *acres of land.*

This is a grant made on the 10th January, 1818. The petitioner, for services, which he tendered a certificate to prove, declares, "That he had purchased 29 Slaves, and requests for said services the donation to which he was entitled, 875 acres, on the West side of Lake George, in a Hammock known as 'Big Spring,' and 150 acres at the same place," for an equal number of acres which he possesses at Matanzas, and of which he makes an absolute abandonment, being in all 1025 acres. The decree is, that he may have the land. This is a good claim; grants for services, should always *be made in proportion to the workers,* and require no evidence of cultivation. It has been surveyed. Confirmed.

No. 41.

FRANCIS PELLICER, *Claimant—2000 acres of land.*

Francis Pellicer petitions the Government for 2000 acres of land, under the Royal order of 29th March, 1815; and by a decree of the 24th January, 1818, Gov. Coppinger grants him 2000 acres at a place called Tomoca, bounded on the North by the lands of Jos. M. Arredondo, on the East by vacant pine land, on the South by the lands of the Heirs of John Russell, and on the West by the public road. On the 22d July, 1818, Governor Coppinger issued to him a Royal Title for the same, and on the 14th March, 1818, Robert McHardy surveys said land for him in the place pointed out. Pellicer sold to Bulow. As this is a bona fide grant, although on the last day, 24th January, 1818, we advise its confirmation.

No. 42.

JOHN MISTRE, *Claimant—50 acres of land.*

In 1816, 100 acres of land was granted to claimant under the order of 1790, and in 1821, a Royal Title was made to him of a small Island, on which Quesada's Battery was built. Confirmed.

No. 43.

PEDRO PESO DE BURGO, *Grantee.*

JOHN A. CAVEDO, (present) *Claimant—200 acres of land.*

In February 1803, Governor White conceded this land at Mosquetto wharf, "running thence South for head rights;" two witnesses have deposed that they saw the grantee living on the tract in 1811, with houses and a crop. We are willing to presume a further residence, and confirm the claim.

No. 44.

J. H. McINTOSH, *Claimant—800 acres of land.*

Mulberry Grove on the St. Johns river, a Royal title made in 1805, by Gov. White to Timothy Hollingsworth, and a conveyance by grantee to claimant, dated 2d May, of the same year. It is confirmed.

No. 45.

JUAN SEGUI, *Claimant*—107 *acres of land.*

This land is situated on the North river, at a place called San Ignacio, and is founded on a Royal title made by Governor White, on the 5th September, 1807, in favor of Lazaro Ortega, who sold the same to present claimant, by deed, bearing date 29th April, 1809. It is confirmed.

No. 46.

DANIEL HURLBERT, *Claimant*—300 *acres of land.*

This land is situated to the South of St. Augustine, at a place called Levett, and was sold by order of the Government, on the 11th September, 1820, to Francis P. Sanchez, who sold the same to present claimant on the 12th April, 1823. This claim is similar, in every respect, to No. 28 of this abstract, and is therefore confirmed.

No. 47.

BENJAMIN CHIRES, *Claimant*—300 *acres of land.*

A Royal title made by Governor Kindelan to William Laurence, in 1815, "to 300 acres of land on Amelia Island," based on a concession in 1805, under the Royal order of 1790. Chaires is the purchaser. Confirmed.

No. 48.

JOSEPH BAYA, *Claimant*—130 *acres of land.*

These lands were sold by the Government, on the 6th November, 1792, as the property of Jesse Fish, deceased, and purchased by Antonio Berta, who conveyed the same to Francisco Rovera on the 29th December, 1798, who sold the same to Jose de Zubezarreta on the 30th December, 1799, whose widow, Germana de Saria, sold the same to the present claimant on the 21st June, 1823. It is confirmed.

No. 49.

FRANCIS GOODWIN'S heirs, *Claimants*—640 *acres of land.*

This quantity of land is confirmed to the claimants. For report see No. 68, abstract B.

No. 50.

CYRUS BRIGGS, *Claimant*—250 *acres of land.*

Concession in 1804, on the river Nassau, on Lofton's creek; proof by two witnesses that he cultivated it many years, and that it has never been out of the possession of Ledwith, the grantee, and his representatives. Cyrus Briggs claims for himself, and others, the lawful heirs of Ledwith. It is confirmed.*

No. 51.

CYRUS BRIGGS, *Claimant*—100 *acres of land.*

A concession by Governor White, in June, 1803, for Pearson's Island, about 100 acres; proof of possession by two witnesses, until the latter part of 1813. Confirmed.

No. 52.

WILLIAM DRUMMOND, *Claimant*—400 *acres of land.*

This land lies on the river St. Mary's, at a place called Casa Blanca. It was surveyed to Richard Lang by Pedro Marrot, in 1792, and re-surveyed by George Clarke, in October, 1818. In February, 1816, the claimant, Lang, applied to the Governor, to have a copy of his original concession given him from the office. The Governor directs it to be done, and we consider this, together with the survey of Clarke, sufficient evidence of continued possession. It is confirmed.

No. 53.

HEIRS OF JOS. HAGINS, *Claimant*—200 *acres of land.*

This land was surveyed to Jesse Frost by Pedro Marrot, in 1793. It lies on Julington creek, St. John's river. It appears to the Board, by two depositions in the case, that Jos. Hagins derived the land from Frost by inheritance, and that the parties have lived on it ever since. Confirmed.

No. 54.

THE HEIRS OF THOS. FITCH, *Claimants*—400 *acres of land.*

This land lies on Diego plains, at a place called Levett's plantation. In 1818, this land was in contest before the Judicial tribunal here, between Montes de Oca and Francis X. Sanchez. The Governor adjudged it to be the property of Montes de Oca, and decreed that the full title should be made him. Montes de Oca sold to Geo. Fleming, and Fleming to Thomas Fitch, to whose heirs we confirm it.

* These are the same claims confirmed in the name of the Ledwiths, Michael and Garret. Nos. 36 and 37 of this report.

No. 55.

James McGirt, *Claimant.*

No. 55. 300 *acres land on St. Mary's river.*
No. 56. 300 *do on Nassau river.*
No. 57. 80 *do a small island on St. Mary's river.*

These three cases are reported at length in Nos. 88, 89, and 90, on report marked B.

No 58.

Francis de Medicis, *Claimant*—400 *acres of land on the West side of the North River.*

In 1792, this land was first granted. In 1798, Juan Salon, the original grantee, requested a renewal of his certificate, the first being lost. The certificate was ordered to be renewed accordingly. In 1820, M. Palon, son of John, sold the land to the present claimant before the notary of this city, *Juan de Entralgo.* There is no positive evidence of cultivation in the case. But the sale in 1820, attested before the notary public, or escrivano, we consider sufficient. He was a judicial as well as executive officer, and we believe he was bound, by the nature of his office, to record no deed unless the title was good. We have, therefore, confirmed this claim.

No. 59.

Heirs of Thomas Lamb, *Claimants*—200 *acres of land on Amelia Island.*

The concession is dated on the 25th October, 1798. C. W. Clark deposed that he knows the land called Lamb's Old Field, and that it was a matter of public notoriety that Lamb lived on said land for a number of years. John Uptegrove was, in 1802, upon the land, and Lamb was living there with a large family. It is confirmed.

No. 60.

James Hall, *Claimant*—450 *acres of land.*
No. 61. do do 250 *do.*

These two claims are confirmed to William Craig. See abstract of the Register and Receiver of 1827, Nos. 1 and 2.

No. 62.

E. Hudnall's Heirs, *Claimants*—100 *acres of land.*

The claim of the United States to this land was relinquished by the Board of Commissioners to David Miller. The parties, in this case, as in the preceeding, are left to their action at law.

No. 63.

MARTIN HERNANDEZ, *Claimant—2000 acres of land.*

This land was granted for military services by Gov. Coppinger, on the 16th September, 1817. 500 acres lie in Cyprus Swamp, 1000 at the head of the Northwest Creek, emptying into the river Mantanzas, and 500 on the river Halifax. It is confirmed.

No. 64.

FRANCIS P. SANCHEZ, *Claimant—2000 acres of land.*

This land was granted to Francisco Medicis for military services, in December, 1815, and sold by him to the present claimant in 1823. There is an order of survey made in 1815, which seems never to have been executed. It lies on the river Ocklewaha, and is confirmed.

No. 65.

ACHILLES MURAT, *Claimant—1200 acres of land.*

One thousand acres of this tract was granted, by royal title, in March, 1816, to F. M. Arredondo, jr. It lies on the Mantanzas river, about nine miles South of St. Augustine. It was sold by Arredondo, jr. to Moses E. Levy, and by him sold to the present claimant. The other two hundred acres adjoins the first tract, and is derived from Honoria Clarke, whose title has been fully reported on abstract C, No. 14. This is a part of the land assigned to Margaretta Clarke in the distribution of the estate of her mother Honoria, made in 1809, and fully approved by the Government in 1810. The claim to Murat is confirmed.

No. 66.

MARY DEWEES, *Claimant—500 acres of land.*

This is the same land confirmed to Joseph Dill, No. 6, under whom Dewees claims.

No. 67.

JOSEPH M. SANCHEZ, *Claimant—200 acres of land.*

This land lies on the river Halifax, at Musquitoe, at a place called Sorruguey. It was conceded, by Governor White, to Getrudes Carrillo, in March, 1804. During the year 1821, Francis D. Medicis, as Attorney for Mrs. Carrillo, applied to Governor Coppinger for a royal title; upon full proof before the Governor that she had complied with the conditions of the grant, he directed the title to be made. Sanchez claims under the grant to Carrillo, to whom, Carrillo, the title of the United States is relinquished.

No. 68.

Hannah Smith, *Claimant*—389⅔ *acres of land.*

This land is situated at a place called St. Lucia, on the North river. It is claimed under a royal title, made the 10th July, 1804, to John Andreas, from whose representatives the present claimant has purchased it. Confirmed.

No. 69.

Josiah Smith, *Claimant*—1000 *acres of land.*

On the 10th May, 1815, the land claimed, described to be "pine land," situated on a "tongue" of land between St. Mary's and Bell's rivers, was granted, by Governor Kindelan, to Smith, for services. There is filed, amongst the papers in this claim, a survey without signature or certificate. This concession, like that to Pablo Fontane, Report 2, No. 124, we should consider insufficient to justify us in confirming the claim, and for the reasons there given; but in the year 1820, Governor Coppinger executed a royal title in favor of the claimant, and it is confirmed.

No. 70.

James Ervin, *Claimant*—125 *acres of land.*

Governor White conceded this land on the 2d December, 1803. It is situated on River Little St. Mary's, at the crossing place. The evidence is, the deposition of Geo. J. F. Clarke, that Ervin, the claimant, was in actual cultivation in the years 1809, '10, and '11, and has so continued with small intermissions to the present time. It is confirmed.

No. 71.

Andres Papy, *Claimant*—126 *acres of land.*

On the 13th May, 1793, P. Marrot surveyed this land to Josefa Espinosa; and on the 25th January, 1811, Governor White gave to her a royal title. It was sold by Espinosa to Philip Solana, and by him on the 9th February, 1819, which sale was duly recorded by the Escribano to Anne Pous, under whom Papy claims. It is confirmed. It is situated at a place called Fort San Diego, North St. Augustine.

No. 72.

Edward R. Gibson, *Claimant*—250 *acres of land.*

These lands were conceded by Govenor Coppinger to Joseph Delespine on the 30th July, 1816, by virtue of the royal order of 1790. H. Dexter has proved cultivation and possession in the present claimant, who derives his title from Joseph Delespine, the grantee. The lands lie near Moultrie creek, and are said to be bounded by those granted by Daniel Livinney. Confirmed.

No. 73.

Elizabeth Bunch, *Claimant*—100 *acres of land.*

In 1806, Governor White granted to Samuel Bunch, the deceased husband of the claimant, by concession, one hundred acres of land, situated on the river Halifax, in front of the first key after passing the key called Pellican. One witness has proved long and continued possession of the parties; and the claim is confirmed.

No. 74.

Benjamin Chaires, *Claimant*—300 *acres of land.*

A Royal title made on the 4th July, 1815, by Joseph Estrada, Governor pro tem. to Don Bartolome de Castra y Ferrer, for 300 acres on Amelia Island, at a place called Beiche Hammoc. The land was first conceded in 1802, under the order of 1790. Benjamin Chaires is the present claimant. It is confirmed.

No. 75.

Josiah Smith, *Claimant*—400 *acres of land.*

In 1804, a concession was made to Archibald Atkinson, in the usual manner, from whom Smith claims by purchase, situated at Spell's Old Field, on the North Branch of the river Nassau; John Uptegrove has deposed, that, in that year, he, the deponent, was employed by Atkinson to settle the place. He took with him five or six hands, and put up a log building, suitable for a residence; he says, moreover, that the lands have ever since been claimed by Atkinson and Smith. José Maria Ugarte, deposes that, in 1814, Atkinson having been killed in the service of Spain, his property was directed to be sold by government, for the benefit of his representatives, and at that sale, so sanctioned, the land here claimed was purchased by Smith. This is sufficient to justify us in confirming it.

No. 76.

James Curtis, *Claimant*—400 *acres of land.*

The evidence in this claim is somewhat defective, but, nevertheless, it appears to us to be good. The original British title, on which the claim is founded, has not been filed in the office; but there is a certificate of the Assistant Surveyor General, Benjamin Lord, dated on the 20th May, 1784, to a plat of the land, which plat he certifies to be a true copy of the register plat in the Surveyor General's Land Office in East Florida. The plat and the register aforesaid, bears date 10th September, 1766. In addition to this, there is a deed of bargain and sale from Thomas Brown to James Curtis, the present claimant, made on the 1st August, 1784. Properly, there should have been produced to the board, the original grant made to Stewart, a copy of its register and survey, (which last alone is done) and some evidence to prove, that the sale to Curtis was recognized by the Spanish Government. But, from the length of time which has elapsed since the date of the transaction, from the antiquity of the deed, and from the difficulty of obtaining written and record evidence of British titles, those titles having been removed by the British government in 1783, we cannot expect such rigid proof as would otherwise be required. Curtis is described in the deed from Brown, as a Spanish subject, a Lieutenant in the Hibernian regiment, then in East Florida; and as by the provisions of the treaty in 1783. The British subjects holding lands in Florida, were permitted to sell them within eighteen months, which in the present case, was done. We confirm the claim.

The land is situated on North river and on the West side, about 8 miles from St. Augustine, on the Bluff Point, at a place called Arrenges.

No. 77.

The Heirs of Geo. Long, *Claimant*—600 *acres of land.*

It appears by reference to a list of "inhabitants, with their lands on the river Matanzas, and its settlement," made by the directions of Gov. White, in 1801, that Geo. Long, the father of the present claimants, at that time owned six hundred acres of land. In the memorials of Dupont, of Clarke, and of others, these lands of Long are frequently pointed out as boundaries. These claimants had determined to abandon the claim of their father, and apply for a donation; that application has been reported on report 5, No. 35. It will be seen by reference to the evidence in that case, that Geo. Long cultivated the land from 1801 to 1813, and that his representatives re-possessed themselves of it, as soon as it was safe to do so in 1821. It is therefore a good claim, and we confirm it.

C. DOWNING,
W. H. ALLEN.

LIST OF CLAIMS

CONFIRMED DURING THE YEAR 1828.

REPORT No. 1.—Continued.

REGISTER of Claims to Land in East

Numbers.	Present claimants.	Original claimants.	Date of patent or royal title.	Date of concession or order of survey.	Quantity of land. Acres.
1	Thomas H. Dummett	John Burch	April 4, 1819	Aug. 11, 1804	1168
2	Moses Harrold	Moses Harrold	1807	1821	395
3	Antonio Huertes	Antonio Huertes	1813	- -	800
4	John Burch	Patrick Dean	1819	1804	995
5	Heirs of Roque Leonardy	Heirs of R. Leonardy	1821	1792	1400
6	Heirs of Robert C. Maxcy	Joseph Dell	1821	1803	500
7	F. Falany's executors	F. Falany's executors	1819	1805	1200
8	Benjamin Chaires	Robert Andrew	1809	- -	500
9	John B. Richard's heirs	J. B. Richard's heirs	- -	1803	230
10	James Falany	James Falany	- -	1805	185
11	William Hollingsworth	William Hollingsworth	- -	1803	150
12	Heirs of Rob't Pritchard	Thomas Bowden	- -	1790	250
13	Margaret O'Neil	Margaret O'Neil	1810	- -	300
14	Sarah Foulks	Margaret Jones	- -	- -	100
15	S. Clarke and Js. Brown	Edward Wanton	- -	1801	100
16	Same	Same	- -	1801	650
17	Heirs of Rob't Whitmore	Heirs of R. Whitmore	- -	- -	150
18	James Rose	James Rose	- -	1810	25
19	Margaret O'Neil	Margaret O'Neil	1807	- -	243
20	James Pilot	James Francis Pilot	- -	1803	620
21	Eleanor Pritchard	Eleanor Pritchard	- -	1815	270
22	Francisco Dear Terran	F. D. Terran	- -	Mar. 11, 1797	300
23	Pablo Sabate	P. Sabate	- -	- -	-
24	Francis Richard	Francis Richard	- -	1795	650
25	Isaac Sasportas	I. Sasportas	- -	1817	425
26	George Clark	John Cavado	- -	1801	100
27	Antonio Triay	Antonio Triay	1821	1811	1500
28	David Hurlbert	D. Hurlbert	- -	- -	200
29	W. G. Christopher, adm.	Spicer Christopher	1809	- -	500
30	Philip Solana	Pedro de Cula	- -	Mar. 10, 1807	30
31	John Jones	John Jones	- -	Aug. 26, 1803	100
32	Scipio (a free negro)	Scipio (a free negro)	- -	Oct. 9, 1809	25
33	George J. F. Clarke	G. J. F. Clarke	-	Oct. 7, 1816	1000
34	Heirs of Isaac Lang	Isaac Lang	- -	- -	200
35	Peter Miranda	P. Miranda	July 17, 1816	- -	790
36	Santo Rodriguez	S. Rodriguez	- -	Jan. 24, 1818	200
36	Michael Ledwith	M. Ledwith	- -	1804	250
37	Garret Ledwith	G. Ledwith	-	1803	100
38	George Anderson	Gab. W. Perpall	1816	- -	450
39	Bartholomew Lopez, &c.	Bartholomew Lopez, &c.	- -	- -	17
40	Francis Richard	Francis Richard	- -	Jan. 10, 1818	1025
41	Francis Pelliceer	Francis Pelliceer	July 23, 1818	Jan. 24, 1818	2000

REPORT No. 1.—Continued.

Florida, confirmed during the session of 1828.

By whom conceded.	Authority or royal order under which the concession was granted.	Date of survey.	By whom surveyed.	Where situated. Occupation or cultivation.
White and Coppinger	1790	-	R. M'Hardy	Oak Forest, at Tomoca.
Same	1790	Nv. 30, 1807	John Percal	Nassau river.
Kinderlan - -	1790	-	-	St. Sebastian's river.
White and Coppinger	1790	-	-	West side of Halifax river, and opposite Pelican island.
Quesada & Coppinger	1790	1819	A. Bergevin	On the Pablo road, 15 miles from St. Augustine.
White and Coppinger	1790	-	-	South side of St. John's river.
Quesada & Coppinger	1790	-	-	Tufily, 2 leagues south of St. Augustine.
White - -	1790	-	Ped. Marrot	San Roberto.
White - -	1790	-	-	Head of post Borough creek, St. John's river.
Estrada - -	1790	-	-	Mantanzas river.
- - -	1790	-	-	St. John's river.
Quesada - -	-	-	-	Goodman's lake, St. John's river.
White - -	1790	-	-	Between St. Mary's river and Lanford creek.
- - -	-	1793	Ped. Marrot	Sherson, on the east side of St. John's river.
White - -	1790	-	-	Between Picolata and Solana's plantation.
White - -	1790	-	-	Cedar Hammock.
- - -	-	1792	Ped. Marrot	On the river St. John's, near Goodman's Lake.
White - -	1790	-	-	Pevet's swamp.
White - -	-	-	-	Lanceford creek.
White - -	1790	-	-	Amelia island.
Coppinger - -	1790	-	-	Beauclark's point, St. John's river.
White - -	-	-	-	Amelia island.
- - -	-	-	-	Eight miles from St. Augustine.
Quesada - -	-	-	-	East side of St. John's river.
Coppinger - -	-	-	-	Six mile creek.
White - -	-	-	-	Unana creek, North river.
Coppinger - -	-	-	-	Mouth of river Ocklewaha.
- - -	-	-	-	Five miles from St. Augustine.
- - -	-	-	-	Santa Maria.
White - -	1790	-	-	Moultree, south of St. Augustine.
White - -	1790	-	-	Trout creek.
White - -	1790	-	-	Padanaram, St. John's river.
Coppinger - -	1790	-	A. Burgevin	West side of St. John's river, opposite Picolata.
- - -	-	Mar. 4, 1792	Ped. Marrot	Little St. Mary's river.
Coppinger - -	1815	-	-	River Mantanzas.
Same - -	1815	-	-	St. John's river, Dunn's lake.
White - -	1790	-	-	Nassau river This claim numbered 361 through mistake.
White - -	1790	-	-	Pelot's island.
Kinderlan - -	1790	-	-	Territory of Musquitoe.
- - -	-	-	-	Bridge creek. See Report.
Coppinger - -	1815	-	-	Lake George.
Coppinger - -	1815	-	-	Tomoca.

REPORT No. 1.—Continued.

Numbers.	Present claimants.	Original claimants.	Date of patent or royal title.	Date of concession or order of survey.	Quantity of lands. Acres.
42	John Mestre - -	John Mestre - - -	1821	1816	100
43	John A. Cavedo -	Pedro de Bergos -	-	1803	200
44	I. H. M'Intosh - -	Timo. Hollingsworth -	1805	-	800
45	Juan Segui - -	Lazaro Ortage - -	Sept. 5, 1807	-	107
46	Daniel Hurlbert - -	Frs. P. Sanchez - -	-	-	300
47	Benjamin Chaires -	William Laurence -	1805	1805	300
48	Joseph Baya - -	Jesse Fish - -	-	-	130
49	Francis Goodwin's heirs -	Frs. Goodwin - -	-	-	640
50	Cyrus Briggs - -	Frs. Ledwith - -	-	-	-
51	Cyrus Briggs - -	Garret Ledwith - -			
52	William Drummond -	Richard Laug - -	-	-	400
53	Heirs of Jos. Hagins -	Jesse Frost - -	-	-	200
54	Heirs of Thomas Fitch -	Juan G. Montes de O'ca.	-	-	400
55	James M'Girt - -	James M'Girt - -	-	-	300
56	Same - -	Same - -	-	-	300
57	Same - -	Same - -	-	-	80
58	Francis D. Medicis -	Juan Salan - -	-	1792	400
59	Heirs of Thomas Lamb -	Thomas Lamb - -	-	1798	200
60	James Hall - -	- - -	-	-	450
61	Same - -	- - -	-	-	250
62	Heirs of E. Hudnall -	- - -	-	-	100
63	Martin Hernandez -	M. Hernandez - -	-	Sept. 16, 1817	2000
64	Frs. P. Sanchez -	Frs. D. Medicis - -	-	Decem. 1815	2000
65	Achilles Murat - -	F. M. Arredondo & H. Clark	1816	-	1200
66	Mary Dewees - -	Joseph Dill - -	-	-	500
67	Jos. M. Sanchez -	Gertrudes Carrillo -	1821	March, 1804	200
68	Hannah Smith - -	John Andrio - -	July 10, 1804	-	389⅓
69	Josiah Smith - -	Josiah Smith - -	1820	May 10, 1815	1000
70	James Ervin - -	James Ervin - -	-	Decem. 1803	125
71	Andres Papy - -	Jozefa Espinaza - -	1811	-	126
72	Edward R. Gibson -	James Delespine -	-	July, 1816	250
73	Elizabeth Bunch -	Samuel Bunch - -	-	1806	100
74	Benjamin Chaires -	Barthol. de Castra y Ferrer	July 4, 1815	-	300
75	Josiah Smith - -	Archibald Atkinson -	-	1804	400
76	James Curtis - -	Stewart - - -	-	Sept. 10, 1766	400
77	Heirs of George Long -	George Long - -	-	1801	600

REPORT No. 1.—Continued.

By whom conceded.	Authority or royal order under which the concession was granted.	Date of survey.	By whom surveyed.	Where situated. Occupation or cultivation.
Coppinger - -	1790	-	-	Small island, containing Quesada's battery.
White - -	1790	-	-	Musquitoe wharf.
White - -	1790	-	-	St. John's river.
White -	1790	-	-	North river, Sanigcio.
- - -	-	-	-	At a place called Levet's. See Report.
Kinderlan - -	1790	-	-	Amelia island.
- - -	-	-	-	This land, and Nos. 46 and 47 of this abstract, are claimed by sales of private property made by order of the Government.
- - -	-	-	-	See No 68, Report 2.
- - -	-	-	-	These are the same cases as Nos. 36 and 37 of this report.
- - -	-	1792	P. Marrot -	River St. Mary's, Casablanca.
- - -	-	1793	P. Marrot -	St. John's river, Julington creek.
- - -	-	-	-	On Diego Plains. See Report.
- - -	-	-	-	St. Mary's river,
- - -	-	-	-	Nassau river,
- - -	-	-	-	Small island, on St. Mary's river. Reported at length in Report No. 2, Nos. 88, 89, and 90.
Quesada - -	1790	-	-	West side of the North river.
White - -	1790	-	-	Amelia island.
- -	-	-	-	These two cases have been confirmed to William Craig.
- - -	-	-	-	This land has been confirmed to David Miller.
Coppinger - -	1815	-	-	On Cyprus Swamp, on the river Mantanzas, river Halifax.
Coppinger - -	1815	-	-	Ocklawaha.
Coppinger - -	-	-	-	River Mantanzas, nine miles from St. Augustine.
- - -	-	-	-	This is the same case as No. 6 of this Report.
White and Coppinger	1790	-	-	Halifax river, at a place called Surruguay.
White - -	1790	-	-	St. Lucia, on the North river.
Kinderlan & Coppinger	1815	-	-	Between St. Mary's and Bell's rivers.
White - -	1790	-	-	Little St Mary's river.
White - -	1790	-	-	At Fort San Diego, north of Augustine.
Coppinger - -	1790	-	-	Near Moultree creek.
White - -	1790	-	-	River Halifax.
Estrado - -	1790	-	-	Beiche Hammock, Amelia island.
White - -	1790	-	-	Spell's Old Field, Nassau river.
Tonyn - -	-	-	-	On the west side of the North river, 8 miles from St Augustine, at a place called Arrenges.
White - -	1790	-	-	Mantanzas.

C. DOWNING,
W. H. ALLEN.

REPORT NO. II.

REJECTED CASES.

No. 1.

Bartholomew Suarez, *Claimant—50 acres of land—Moses Creek*

The title for this land is dated 4th August, 1818.

No. 2.

Pablo Sabate, *Claimant—2500 acres of land, west of Casacola.*

Granted by Royal Title, 2d April, 1818.

No. 3.

Estevan Arnau, *Claimant—100 acres of land—Mosquito.*

Royal Title, dated 19th June, 1818.

No. 4.

Thomas Backhouse, *Claimant—500 acres of land—Indian River.*

Grant by Royal Title, 20th June, 1818.

No. 5.

Moses E. Levy, *Claimant—500 acres of land—Indian River.*

Granted by Royal Title, to Joaquin Sanchez, 15th June, 1818.

No. 6.

John Houston, *Claimant—700 acres of land—St. Johns and Nassau.*

Granted by concession, 20th May, 1818.

No. 7.

JOHN GONZALEZ, *Claimant*—1,000 *acres of land*—*St. Diego.*

By Royal Title, 10th June 1818.

No. 8.

F. D. McDOWELL, *Claimant*—800 *acres of land.*

The Claimant produces here, as his only evidence of title, a Certificate of Entralgo, of the 24th May, 1819, stating that the Claimant had no lands precedent to that date.

No. 9.

OCTAVIUS MITCHELL, *Claimant*—2,000 *acres of land*—*Mosquito.*

Claims by Concession, under date 2d June, 1818.

No. 10.

WILLIAM T. HALL, *Claimant*—2,000 *acres of land*—*Mosquito.*

Claims by Concession, 20th October, 1819.

No. 11.

FLORA LESLIE, *Claimant*—500 *acres of land*—*Springer's Branch.*

This Claim is predicated on a Certificate of Thomas De Aguilar, of the 12th April, 1810, the original of which is not to be found in the Office of the Public Archives; and, as Claimant has never proved possession or cultivation of the same, it is rejected.

No. 12.

SUSANNA ROLLINS, *Claimant*—200 *acres of land*—*Nassau.*

This Concession is dated 1799. In 1801, there was a general survey on Nassau; and this person is not named. With no proof of cultivation, the claim must be rejected.

No. 13.

ISABELLA WIGGINS, *Claimant*—300 *acres of land*—*Luke George.*

This is a Claim under the Certificate of George I. F. Clarke, of the 23d March, 1821, with no other document.

No. 14.

J. H. McIntosh, *Claimant.—Quantity undefined—River Miami.*

The original grantee, John McQueen, petitions the Government for 2000 acres of land on the Miami, on the 29th of October, 1795; and on the 5th November, 1795, Governor Quesada gives permission to said grantee, to establish himself on said lands; but as to the number of acres, "there should be assigned to him, the quantity he was entitled to, as soon as the general survey took place:" there is no proof before the Board of the survey, or the possession or cultivation of said land; it is therefore rejected.

No. 15.

Hannah Nobles, *Claimant—1000 acres of land—Lake St. Marks.*

This is a certificate of John de Pierra of the 3d July, 1799, for 1000 acres of land, granted Robert Cowen, the original grantee, by Governor White, on the 2d same month and year, but as neither the original grantee nor present claimant, have proved possession, the claim is rejected.

No. 16.

Thomas Suarez, *Administrator of* Anthony Suarez, *Claimant.*—500 *acres of land—Mills' Swamp.*

The only document presented in this claim is a certificate of survey, of George I. F. Clarke, dated 1st March, 1817. No other proof—rejected.

No. 17.

Abner Williams *heirs, Claimants.—150 acres of land—River St. Johns.*

Agreeably to the certificate of John de Pierra, dated 20th June, 1801, Anastacio Mombromaty petitions Governor White for the above quantity of land, which is granted him. There is no proof of possession by either of the parties; it is therefore rejected.

No. 18.

Edward R. Gibson, *Claimant.—125 acres of land—Moultrie Creek.*

Founded on one of Thomas De Aguilar's certificates, dated 1st July, 1815, with no proof of cultivation or possession. Rejected.

No. 19.

GEORGE MORRISON, *Claimant*—150 *acres of land*—*St. Mary's river*.

This is a certificate of John De Pierra, dated 2nd May, 1805. There is no evidence before the Board of the performance of the conditions contained in said grant; it is rejected.

No. 20.

CHARLOTTE GOBERT, *Claimant*—100 *acres of land*—*St. Marks' Pond.*

This claim is founded on a concession made to Charles, a free Negro, in 1806, with conditions "that he settle in the term of one month." There is no testimony whatever adduced, therefore it is rejected.

No. 21

DANIEL HURLBERT, *Claimant*—125 *acres of land*—*Pevet's Swamp.*

Conceded to claimant on the 3d September 1805, under the royal ordinance of 1790, with the additional condition "that he take possession of the land in one month from the date of the decree." There is no evidence of the performance of the conditions either expressed or implied.

No. 22.

JOSEPH CONE, *Claimant*—115 *acres of land*—*St. Mary's River.*

Conceded on the 29th May, 1805, with conditions similar to those of No. 21. There is no evidence, and the claim is rejected.

No. 23.

ROBERT HUTCHINSON, *Claimant*—450 *acres of land*—*Little St. Mary's River.*

Conceded on the 8th May, 1816, under the Royal order, 1790. Claimant proves nothing, and it is, therefore, rejected.

No. 24.

The Heirs of ROBERT ANDREW, *Claimants*—100 *acres of land.*

On the 3d of October, 1793, R. Andrew petitions the Governor, Quesada, for permission to exchange the lands which were surveyed to him on the plains of St. Diego for an equal quantity on the Savannah of Urlieche; which request was granted, on the 18th of the same month and year: but, as there is no proof before the Board of his ever having taken possession of the same, it is rejected.

No. 25.

Isabella Wiggins, *Claimant—300 acres of land, East of Lake George.*

No evidence of cultivation; it is, therefore, rejected.

No. 26.

Josiah Starkey's *Trustee, Claimant—455 acres of land, St. Mary's River.*

In the memorial of the claimant to the Board he speaks of a concession from Governor Coppinger, which is not produced. There is nothing in the papers but a survey, by George Clarke, and a mortgage, from Charles Sibbald. There is no evidence of cultivation or possession; and the claim is rejected.

Note.—We believe this is the same land confirmed to Charles Sibbald, in a former session of the Board If so, the party will sustain no injury by failing to file his title in this case.

No. 27.

Joseph F. White, *Claimant—250 acres of land.*

Concession made by Gov. White, on the 28th July, 1803, to Alexander Watson, on condition "that he takes possession of the land within six months." In June, 1804, the Governor is satisfied, by evidence, that the land was possessed within the six months specified, and directs a survey. Watson sells to White in 1820. There is no evidence before the Board of the ten years' cultivation by the party, made necessary by the ordinance of 1790, under which the land was granted. It is rejected.

No. 28.

Robert Andrew, *Claimant—100 acres of land.*

Conceded on the 18th November, 1799. He has produced no evidence whatever to justify the Board in confirming his claim.

No. 29.

Daniel C. Hart, *Claimant—150 acres of land.*

Concession, dated 8th January, 1818, certified by Aguilar, and no original in the office. Without any evidence of cultivation, it must be rejected.

No. 30.

William Barden, *Claimant—50 acres of land.*

Conceded on the 6th May, 1805. It is proved, by James Barden, that, in August, the same year, the party was in possession of the land, and making a crop upon it. The Board consider that, when, under the order of 1790, ten years' possession was neccessary to complete a title, they cannot be justified in confirming a claim, one years' possession of which alone is proved.

No. 31.

James Lewis, Jr. *Claimant—50 acres of land.*

Conceded 22d December, 1806, on the condition, " That he take possession of the same in one month." He has proved nothing, and the claim is rejected.

No. 32.

The Widow of Thomas Collier, *Claimant—1200 acres of land.*

Concession dated 8th May, 1804. The condition the same as in the preceding claims, without proof.

No. 33.

Delia Broadoway, *Claimant—500 acres of land.*

Thomas Aguilar's certificate, the 16th September, 1815. The original of which, if there was ever any, is not in the office. No proof of cultivation. The claim is rejected.

No. 34.

Antonio Williams, *(Free Negro) Claimant—300 acres of land.*

Concession dated the 1st December, 1801. Without any proof whatever.

No. 35.

Albany Fallis, *Claimant—50 acres of land.*

Juan De Pierra, Secretary of Government, by Thomas de Aguilar, certifies, " That, to a memorial presented by Albany Fallis, soliciting the number of acres he is entitled to, situated on a small island in the river Nassau. The following decree was made by Gov. White, on the 6th November, 1805:

"Let there be granted to this interested, fifty acres in the place he solicits, which are those he is entitled to, agreeably to his oath, being well understood, that he must establish himself on said land, in the term of one month, counted from the date." No evidence—rejected.

No. 36.

MICHAEL LYNCH, *Claimant—335 acres of land.*

This land was granted on the 22d of June, 1805, under the order of 1790, with the condition, "that he take possession of the same within six months from the date." Nothing is proved, and the claim is rejected.

No. 37.

JOHN G. RUSHING, *Claimant—80 acres of land.*

No title produced, but George Clark's survey and certificate of the 8th February, 1815. There is no proof of cultivation, and the claim is rejected.

No. 38.

EZEKIEL HUDNALL'S HEIRS, *Claimants—900 acres of land.*

This claim is based on concession, dated 3d June, 1817, with the condition, "That they take possession of it within four months." In April, 1821, there is a certificate and survey of George Clark. So far from proving a performance of the conditions, a witness, Samuel Kinsley, has been introduced by the claimants, who proves directly the reverse, and deposes, in a conversation with said Hudnall, that he, Hudnall, declared the fear of the Indians prevented his possession of the land. Hudnall is now dead, and, whilst alive, he was afraid to take possession of the land. By the condition of the grant, his heirs must lose it.

No. 39.

THOMAS ANDREW, *Claimant—200 acres of land.*

Concession on the 23d November, 1803, on the condition, "That he take possession of the land within one month from the date." He has adduced no evidence, and his claim is rejected.

No. 40.

H. B. MARTIN, *Claimant—400 acres of land.*

Conceded on the 3d September, 1803, on the condition, that he take possession within six months. There is no proof, and the claim is rejected.

No. 41.

THOMAS MURPHEY, *Claimant*—3,000 *acres of land.*

An island in the St. John's river. The concession is dated on the 11th June, 1818. It is barred by the treaty.

No. 42.

WILLIAM HART, *Claimant*—1,400 *acres of land.*

In 1811, William Hart applied to the Governor for an indefinite number of acres, on the River St. John's, "to establish a cowpen, for the security of stock." The Governor directed Don Will Craig, a Justice of the Peace, to report "on the propriety of the petition as well as on the number of the stock of said Hart." This was never done, nor was any grant made to the land. It is true that the representatives of the claimant, in their memorial to the Board, have declared that the grant to the land was lost in 1820, in the River St. John's, when their father was drowned; but of this there was no proof; and, as the claim stands, it is a bad one.

No. 43.

JOSEPH B. REYES, *Claimant*—1,700 *acres of land.*

This claim is based upon Thomas Aguilar's unsupported certificate, without evidence of cultivation or possession, or existence and loss of the original. It is rejected.

No. 44.

LEWIS PIKE'S HEIRS, *Claimants*—400 *acres of land.*

In 1801 the claimant petitioned for lands without specifying the number of acres. Governor White made the following decree: "Let there be granted to this party the land which he solicits, and until, according to the number of his family, there shall be measured the quantity he is entitled to." The land is left undefined in quantity, and as there is no evidence of possession, the claim is rejected.

No. 45.

JOHN CREIGHTON, *Claimant*—305 *acres of land.*

Concession on the 29th October, 1803, on the condition, "that he take possession within one month." He has adduced no proof before the Board, and the claim is rejected.

No. 46.

George Webber, *Claimant—100 acres of land.*

Concession on the 21st January, 1804. Conditioned, that he take possession of the same within one month. There is no proof, and the claim is rejected.

No. 47.

Thomas Yonge, *Claimant—1,100 acres of land.*

Concession dated the 23d July, 1803, on the condition, "That he take possession within six months." There is no proof of performance, and the claim is rejected.

No. 48.

The Heirs of Nathaniel Hall, *Claimant.*

This claim is founded on a simple concession, made by Governor White, 27th July, 1799. There is no proof of possession, or any other evidence before the Board; and it is therefore rejected.

No. 49.

Elias B. Gould, *Claimant—500 acres of land.*

This is a part of a grant to George J. F. Clarke, of four thousand acres. See report No. 12, claim No. 5, where it is reported on at length.

No. 50.

The heirs of Augustine Dimillere, *Claimants—170 acres of land.*

Rejected for the want of proof.

No. 51.

Francisco Paz, *Claimant—1500 acres of land.*

On the 12th November, 1815, Thomas Aguilar certifies, that fifteen hundred acres of land were granted to the claimant on the Palecco Creek for his merits and services under the provisions of the ordinance of 1815. The original of this certificate is not in the office of the public archives. It is rejected.

No. 52.

JAMES DELL, *Claimant—500 acres of land.*

This is another certificate of Thomas Aguilar's, dated 1816. It does not appear whether the grant was made under the ordinance of 1790, or under that of 1815. If under the first, the claimant should have proved possession, which he has not done, and we cannot suppose it was a grant for services, when the claimant was one of the most distinguished leaders of the rebels. It is rejected.

No. 53.

The heirs of JOHN FAULK, *Claimants—250 acres of land.*

This claim is based on a certificate of Aguilar's, dated 1817. "That on the 20th June, 1792, Quesada granted this land to the claimant, situated on a place called Andivion's Cowpen, on St. Mary's River." He has produced no evidence to prove possession, and moreover, it appears by the examination of Don Pedro Marrot's survey, dated the 20th June, 1792, that other lands had been surveyed to this party at a place called "*Lime Spring*," on the same river. Of this survey no mention has been made in the memorial or decree presented to the Board, and it seems strange, if this certificate be not a forgery, that Faulk should have petitioned for lands to the Governor, when, on the same day, other lands had been surveyed by Marrot. It is rejected.

No. 54.

FREDERICK HARTLEY, *Claimant—400 acres of land.*

This case has been acted on and rejected by the former Board. It appears by the affidavit of James Simerall, that he was compelled by the Spanish Government to move from this place in consequence of the Revolution, and other lands have been granted to him in lieu of this.

No. 55.

ANDREW DROUILLARD, *Claimant—3000 acres of land.*

On the 10th January, 1818, the claimant petitioned and obtained leave of Governor Coppinger, to change the location of lands that had been granted him in the preceding year, to the North of Dun's Lake, at a place called Oldfield. The grant is incumbered with these conditions, "that as soon as he proves possession of the land, cultivation without intermission, and that he has built the necessary houses and fences, there shall be issued to him a title of property agreeably to the survey which the surveyor may present." On the 15th of April succeeding, the land was surveyed by Clarke, but it does not appear that any proof was adduced to the Governor, and none is before us, to shew that either of the preceding conditions was complied with. It is rejected.

No. 56.

WILLIAM HULL, *Claimant—500 acres of land.*

Concession made, the 1st March, 1792, to "that quantity of land which may correspond to himself and family." The Governor directs that Don Pedro Marrot may proceed to survey to the petitioner, "as much land as he and his family may be entitled to." There is no plat of a survey filed before the Board, nor does Hull's name appear on the list of inhabitants upon the river St. Johns, to whom lands had been surveyed by Marrot. The number of 500 acres assumed as the amount of the grant is entirely gratuitous, as the number to which he was entitled was directed to be specified by a survey, which was never made. It is rejected.

No. 57.

JOSEPH MILLS, *Claimant—200 acres of land.*

This claim is founded on a bare memorial, of the 15th February, 1793, to which Gov. Quesada makes the following decree, on the same day, month, and year: "With respect to what the party sets forth, should nothing against it occur to the officer charged with the distribution of lands, let the quantity wanting to complete what his family is entitled to, be granted to him, in the place which he points out." As the claimant has never produced a plat of the survey of the same, or proof that he cultivated the land, we are of opinion that it should be rejected.

No. 58

WILLIAM ULMER, *Claimant—200 acres of land.*

William Ulmer petitioned the Government, on the 15th September, 1803, "for two hundred acres of land situated at Musquitoe, about 10 miles from New Smyrna, which place was owned during the British dominion, by John Tenant:" to which, Governor White made the following decree, on the same day, month, and year: "Let there be granted to this party the 200 acres of land which he solicits, without injury to a third person, and until, according to the number of workers he may have for the cultivation thereof, there shall be measured what he is entitled to, being well understood, that he must take possession of the said land in the term of six months, counted from the date of this decree." There is no evidence, and the claim is rejected.

No. 59.

DAVID TURNER, *Claimant—90 acres of land.*

By the certificate of John de Pierra, dated 3d February, 1809, David Turner petitions the Government for lands under the royal order of 1790, (setting forth the number of his family and slaves) which is acceded to by Gov. White, who grants him 90 acres, but with the express condition that he shall "establish himself on said land within the term of one month." There is no proof before us of the compliance with this condition, and it is therefore rejected.

No. 60.

Pollard McCormock, *Claimant—2000 acres of land.*

On the 11th July, 1803, McCormock petitioned for 2000 acres of land at Tomoka, under the order of 1790. Two days afterwards, the Governor having heard the report of the engineer, gives him the land on condition that he take possession within six months. On the third October, 1803, the claimant represents to the Governor that he has not taken possession of the land, in consequence of constant bad weather, and begs that John Purcell may be directed to survey the lands. The Governor granted the request, with the express condition that the survey of Purcell should not exempt the land from forfeiture, in the event that the claimant did not take possession of them, with a sufficient number of workers to correspond with the number of acres granted, within the six months from the date of the concession. There is no survey and no evidence that he ever took possession. It is rejected.

No. 61.

William Ladd, *Claimant—1525 acres of land.*

John de Pierra certifies, that on the 3d January, 1804, the lands claimed were granted by Gov. White, on the condition "that he take possession of the same within six months from the date." He has adduced no proof, and his claim is rejected.

No. 62.

Hibberson and Yonge, *Claimants—2000 acres of land.*

On the 23d February, 1815, Gov. Coppinger granted to Hibberson and Yonge, 2000 acres of land on St. Mary's river, "with the understanding that as soon as the survey and plat of said land shall be presented to them, and they prove having cultivated and improved them in a proper manner, the title and absolute property shall be despatched to them." In the succeeding year, Joseph M. Hernandez, as a quit for the claimants, petitioned the Governor to change the location of one thousand acres of the grant, to a place called "Trout Creek Swamp." The change is permitted, and in 1816, George Clarke certified that he had surveyed 1000 acres of land on Trout Creek Swamp; and in 1821, he further certifies, "that he surveyed another thousand at the same place, which latter change had been permitted by Government, on the 20th June of the same year." This last decree is not amongst the papers. It does not appear that either of the tracts were possessed or cultivated by the claimant, and if there be any title whatever, to the second tract of one thousand acres on Trout Creek Swamp, surveyed by George Clarke, in 1821, it passed by the decree of the Governor after his power had ceased, under the treaty. They are both bad.

No 63.

JAMES PELOT, *Claimant*—496 *acres of land.*

No. 64.

JAMES PELOT, *Claimant*—356 *acres of land.*

It seems by the papers before the board, that Pedro Marrot surveyed to James Pelot, the two tracts of land above claimed, one at a place called Pelot, on the River St. John's, and the other at *Pumpkin Bluff*, on Nassau, in the year 1793. There is no evidence before the Board that he possessed or cultivated these lands, but we are fully satisfied, that 640 acres on Amelia Island, were granted to the claimant in lieu of these two surveys. These 640 acres have been confirmed; and in the decree of confirmation, No. 20, of abstract No. 1, will be found more at large our views upon this subject.

No. 65

JOSIAH DUPONT'S HEIRS, AND GIDEON DUPONT, *claim, viz:*

No. 1.	1850 acres	of Land.
" 2.	500 acres	
" 3.	500 acres	
" 4.	1400 acres	

On the 18th August, 1792, Josiah Dupont, a new settler, prays for "one half of the quantity of acres of land, corresponding to himself, his wife, 5 daughters, 2 sons, and 27 slaves, upon the head of the East water stream, ten miles South of the Fort Mantanzas," and the other half on the head of a stream called Graham, adjoining the lands of Jesse Fish, and adds: "That the lands described are the same where he is now settled, by the verbal permission of the Governor."

The decree is, "That he may remain where he is established, permitting him at the same time to augment to the quantity of land to which he is entitled, *according to the regulations of this Government*, in the place called Graham's Creek," &c. "and until the general survey which is *now* taking place, *when he will receive his complement of which he will remain proprietor.*"

QUESADA.

This is on the 31st August. The general survey of 1792, extended to Mantanzas.

The second claim is based on a concession of Quesada, dated the 18th Oct. 1794. Dupont, in his memorial, says to the Governor, "that his force being so large, he cannot take his lands in one place---That his Excellency had already granted him one thousand acres of Rice land, one hundred in the large Orange Grove, and he wishes permission to take five hundred more, to complete his complement between the lands of Travers, Cartel Palisier, and Clark." The Governor grants the request, "until the final survey takes place for the quantity corresponding to his force." There was no survey until 1801.

The third claim is this: In July, 1801, the 28th, Dupont petitioned for five hundred acres of land more, in Graham's Swamp. The Engineer's report is favorable, and White, on the 29th July, of the same year, granted the lands "until his due complement should be surveyed."

Fourth. Don Gideon Dupont, on the 27th May, 1802, makes application to the Governor "for 700 acres of land in Graham's Swamp." "Bounded on the South by those lately granted to his father, Josiah Dupont." "And the petitioner to make his settlement as soon as the irruptions of the savages shall have ceased," "and in addition to the 700 acres, *also* the intervening spaces."

"The Engineer, to whom the subject is referred, reported, that there existed a difficulty—that *this land* is solicited by Josiah Dupont, under date of the 28th July 1801, and by George Long, on the 7th October, same year."

He then adds: "But 700 acres and 700 acres more of intervening space, are 1400 acres ceded to a person, who, according to what I have heard, has not sufficient property to cover it according to the regulations." "And this I am of opinion of, that the most that ought to be granted him is 200 acres with the intervening space."

The decree of the Governor, after the party had taken the oath of allegiance, is this: "Let the prayer of the petitioner be granted, without injury, &c. and *until*, according to the force he possesses, the corresponding quantity of land be surveyed." This decree is dated the 3d June, 1802. It may be well to remark that these are the same lands, petitioned for by his father in the above case No. 3, and that this Gideon Dupont now claims them to be different tracts, asks confirmation of 500 acres, No. 3, as heir of Josiah, and 1400, as bounding the former for himself. Long, who by the report of the Engineer was a conflicting claimant, appears by the survey of Marrot in 1801, to have had allotted to him 600 acres, and that claim is now before the Board.

It is unnecessary to comment on the fraudulent attempt to impose on this Board, by making separate, duplicate concessions to the same land, and claiming as a second grant a mere copy of the first, so as to obtain a double quantity.

The evidence in support of the three first claims, is the affidavit of C. W Clarke. He swears, that Josiah Dupont "lived at a place called Murrits' Old Field, at the head of the east prong of Mantanzas river," and continued to live there, and to cultivate the land, until about the beginning of the year 1802, when the Indians came and carried off his negroes, &c. That Dupont had between 30 and 40 working hands and several hundred head of cattle. That when Dupont was driven from the place, one Hughes and two old negroes were left by him, in care of, &c. He adds that Dupont's negroes were never reclaimed from the Indians.

There is a letter to the Board, filed in September, 1824, from Joseph M. Hernandez, claiming most of the above land, and tendering proof, when called on, that Dupont had forfeited his title. He was never called on.

Upon the examination of the surveys made by Don Pedro Marrot at Mantanzas, in 1801, in January, Dupont's name does not appear. In each of the cases above, this survey is made a prerequisite to a consummation of his title. It was indispensably necessary to settle and define the quantity of acres to which he was entitled.

From the instructions given to Marrot (1791) each party to whom lands were surveyed should take an oath as to the number of his family. In the 6th article of instructions, he is directed to "give notice very particularly to all the grantees, that they have to perform certain requisites, before they can be considered as possessed of a full title and be able to dispose of what is now given them." "He shall send them to the office of the Secretary of Government for their respective titles, when they will receive the necessary information."

It is evident that *the title*, which must be obtained after the survey is made, differs from *the title* by concession such as is produced by the claimants in this case, for in the first article of his instructions, Marrot is directed to make the surveys "*limiting himself to the title.*"

Dupont's name, as we have said, does not appear in the survey on Mantanzas in 1801, the only one ever made there. It would seem he had not abandoned the country; because the date of the survey is in January, and one of his memorials is dated in July of the same year. But it is certain that if he still remained in the province, he neglected to have his lands included in the general survey. Without which, by the positive provisions of the grant *itself*, the title could not be perfected. When lands are given gratuitously, and slight conditions, mostly formal, are imposed, and the party fails or refuses to comply with them, he cannot complain if they are lost.

The quantity to which he was entitled depended on the number of his workers, and this number he was required to verify on oath. This he has failed to do; he has not given to the Government the evidence required to authorize the grant. He has not had his limits defined, when a surveyor was sent for that purpose to the spot, nor procured the full title, prescribed in the regulations; nor does it appear that he has lived out the ten years, without which his title is unquestionably bad. If we do not receive the omission of his name, on the surveys of Marrot in January, 1801, as it is, perhaps, our duty to do, as conclusive evidence to show the abandonment, it is because, in July of the same year, his third petition to the Governor contradicts the presumption; but still, *his time* would not be completed in July, and his failure to comply with the conditions of the grant, by having it surveyed, and the deficiency of the proof of continued possession, if there were no other papers in the cause, would prevent a confirmation of these claims. The most of these lands have been granted to others at subsequent periods, and so far as they have been re-granted, the claim of the United States has been already relinquished by the Board of Commissioners, and our investigation of these cases would be a useless labor. But, it may not be, that all the lands claimed by the heirs of Dupont are granted and confirmed to others. And for this résidue, if any there be, we are driven to act on these cases.

It should be presumed, that the agents of a foreign Government had done their duty, and not injustice, by giving away lands already the property of another, and nothing is produced by Dupont to rebut this presumption.

But this matter is not left to presumption. In 1805, Governor White directed a letter to the Captain General of Cuba, of which the following is an extract: "Surprised to see that Dupont considered himself to have a just title to reclaim lands, which, if his father, by going to the United States, had not abandoned, would not be hereditary, until after ten years of uninterrupted cultivation, they are conceded to the grantees in absolute property: in which respect Dupont is deficient; and convinced that, to listen to such pretensions, would give occasion to numberless law suits, disturbing the quiet of good and bona fide settlers, who would not feel secured in their lands, even though they had possessed and cultivated them for successive years, and built houses on them. The circumstances, under which this individual claims, are particularly objectionable, as, after having taken the oath of allegiance on the 3d June, 1802, and having granted to him, on the same day, seven hundred acres of land, for twenty-five negroes, which he offered to introduce into the Province, he returned to the United States, where he has constantly resided with his mother and sisters, and returned here solely for the purpose of asking for the lands of his father, and selling them, as he explains in his petitions, not with a view of establishing himself in the Province, as is proved by his not having negroes in it, or having brought with him even one of the twenty-five, which he offered." It may be further remarked, that the greater part of the lands claimed by Dupont were formerly granted to others. And attending to such pretensions as his, would be the cause of hindering individuals from asking for lands although they should see them uncultivated; but they might be dispossessed of them, or exposed to an expensive law suit." After this, we may be permitted to express our surprise, that the Duponts should come before this Board. The four claims are rejected.

No. 66.

THE HEIRS OF PHILIP DILL, } *Claimants*—800 *acres of land.*
JOHN H. MCINTOSH, }

This is the same tract of land claimed by both, for the benefit of McIntosh. In 1801, on the petition of Philip Dill "for a plantation on the West side of the River St. John's, abandoned by Francis Richard, as well as another adjoining it, containing in all eight hundred acres." Governor White decreed, that the lands be granted, and until according to the number of his family, &c.

Sometimes it may be inferred, that the conditions on which every grant under the order of 1790 was made, viz: ten years' cultivation, have been complied with; and that the lapse of time, two intervening rebellions, and a partial change of population, always incident to a transfer of a province from one Government to another, may prevent the possibility of obtaining proofs, otherwise easy of access. Here nothing is left to conjecture. The witnesses produced by the claimants, have reduced it to a certainty, that Dill resided on the land at most but three years. Seymour Pickett says, "Dill settled land in 1802, lived on it about two years and removed to the Bluff, where he died, and that none of his family, so far as he believes, ever moved back to the place."

Isaac Hendricks deposes, that Dill resided on the place about 3 years and died. That the family, on the death of Dill, gathered in the crop, and moved to Pittsburg, the said land, as witness understood, having been sold." McIntosh has produced a deed from James Dill, to this land, dated 1805. McIntosh gives as a reason to the Board, for not obtaining Royal titles, the insurrection in 1812; but nothing prevented his showing to this Board that he had performed the implied conditions of the grant, and thereby became entitled to them.

We have too often, expressed our opinion on cases similar to this, to be at a loss to decide. Gov. White, in his letter, in the case of Dupont, expressly says, that lands cannot be inherited until the ten years are lived out." It is then in the power of the heirs to complete the term and perfect the title: and it is, in more than one decree, declared, "That they cannot be alienated without the permission of the Government." Here there was an abandonment, and a sale in three years. If one could not forfeit his lands by abandonment, this tract would belong to Francis Richard, to whom, as appears by the memorial of the party himself, it had been previously granted. He obtained it there, by the abandonment of Richard, and by his own abandonment, he must lose it. If McIntosh, his transferee, had cultivated the land on the sale, something might be left to inference, from the acquiescence of the Government, but on this there is no proof, and it is rejected.

No. 67.

CLARISSA FISH, *Claimant*—150 *acres of Land.*

Claimant purchased of Andrew Campbell in 1821. To Campbell this land was granted by concession in 1804. One witness knew that the land was cultivated in 1805. One year's occupancy will not give a title. It is rejected.

No. 68.

FRANCIS GOODWIN'S HEIRS, *Claimants*—1300 *acres of land.*—1300 *acres of land.*—640 *acres of land.*

The first claim is to land on Pablo Creek, on concession dated in October 1791. He prays to be permitted to establish himself on Pablo—and that a grant be made him of the acres corresponding to the number set forth, viz. a wife, 3 children, and 19 negroes. In Feb 1792, he prays, that the number of acres "which correspond to himself, three children and, 19 negroes," may be granted, "on the plantation which, under the British Government, belonged to one Baileys, four miles south of one St. Vincent Ferrer, &c."

The decree of the Governor is the same in both cases. It in *the first* permits the party to be established for *the present*, on the land, until, in the general survey which is about taking place, there shall be measured to him, the No. of acres that correspond to his family, of which he shall be put in possession, with the corresponding title."

In the second, the Governor says, "agreeably to the request, for which purpose, let the memorial be passed to the Captain Don Pedro Marrot, charged with the general distribution of lands, until he measure to this party, those corresponding to this family in the place he points out." Goodwin then had changed his wish to locate on Pablo, and obtained leave to settle elsewhere. The Governor permitted the change, and directed him to have the quantity, which Marrot should ascertain on the oath of the party to be the portion to which he was entitled.

In May, 1792, Marrot surveyed to Goodwin, at the place mentioned in the second memorial, the land to which he was entitled, by the number of his family, under the proceeding decrees of Quesada, to wit, 640.

Goodwin now, by his representatives, claims the whole three, making 3240 acres. It would be well if so glaring an effort at imposition could be punished by the loss of the whole claim. But Mr. Hendrics having proved that he lived on the survey of Marrot No. 3, at a place called Strawbury, by which name it is also called in the survey up to 1805, this last tract of 640 acres, is confirmed, and the other two are rejected.

No. 69.

JOHN LOVE, *Claimant—300 acres of land.*

This is an old British grant, 1772, of lands 15 miles south of St. Augustine, and a survey in 1781. The claimant has produced to the Board his evidence of citizenship in South Carolina, in 1798. This grant was never recognized by the Spanish Government, and by proving himself a citizen of the United States, he has proved that he has no title to this land. It is rejected.

No. 70.

GEORGE TILLET, *Claimant—250 acres of land.*

This claim is evidenced by Marrot's survey in 1792, on Trout Creek; in 1801 on Marrot's second survey, or rather list of inhabitants on the St. John's, Tillet's name is not to be found. It is therefore to be presumed that he had abandoned the place. It is rejected.

No. 71.

FRANCIS P. SANCHEZ, *Claimant—2,000 acres of land.*

This is a certificate of Thomas D. Aguilar, that in December, 1815, Estrada granted Don John Perchman, Cornet of the Squadron of Dragoons, for services, 2,000 acres of land, at a place called Ockliwaha, on the St. John's River.

In 1819, Perchman sold to Sanchez. In the memorial of the claimant to this Board, he speaks of a survey made by authority in 1819. If this had been produced, it would have furnished some support to the certificate of Aguilar. As it is, we reject the claim.

No. 72.

HIBBERSON & YONGE, *Claimants—2,000 acres of land.*

In 1815, Hibberson & Yonge representing to the Governor that they had greatly improved the country as merchants, and benefited the Treasury by the payment of duties, say, "That they mean to devote themselves to agriculture, and pray the donation of 2,000 acres of land on the River St. Mary's, in absolute property, provided they cultivate them, and improve them, in a proper manner; for which titles may be expedited as soon as surveys are presented in due form; and if your excellency does not determine to conform to these terms, that they may be granted to them on the same terms as they have been granted to the other new settlers, at all times."

The Governor's grant is "with the understanding that, as soon as the survey and plat of said land shall be presented to them, and they prove having cultivated and improved them in a proper manner, a title shall be given," &c. Signed, Kindelan.

On the 16th February, 1816, Joseph M. Hernandez, as the agent of Hibberson & Yonge, represented that the lands on the St. Mary's River, conceded as above, were not vacant, wherefore he "prays permission to locate one thousand acres on Trout Creek Swamp, reserving to himself the right to locate the other thousand acres elsewhere too, if necessary." The Governor permitted the exchange, and cancelled the grant of one thousand acres on the River St. Mary's.

In 1821, Hernandez obtained leave to locate the whole on Trout Creek, in Twelve Mile Swamp, with an order of survey in that place.

It appears by the certificate of George Clarke, in 1820, that he had then surveyed one tract of a thousand acres on Trout Creek. No survey was ever made of the other tract of 1,000 acres, either on St. Mary's or on Trout Creek. The decree of the Governor required that the parties should produce proof of cultivation before a title would be given. And we require the same. There is no evidence that the claimants settled the land, and it must be rejected.

No. 73.

JOHN BELLAMY, *Claimant—500 acres of land.**

This land is situated on McGirt's Creek, and the only document presented to this Board is, a survey, made by George I. F. Clarke, on the 28th October, 1820; it is therefore barred by the Treaty.

No. 74.

SUSANNA CASHEN, *Claimant—300 acres of land, on the River St. John's.*

The only evidence of title filed in this case, is the survey of Andrew Burgevin, dated 1821. It is rejected.

No. 75.

JOHN D. KEHR, *Claimant—300 acres of land on Amelia Island.*

John D. Pierra, in 1801, certifies "that on the application of the claimant, 300 acres of land were granted him on Amelia Island, in three separate tracts, of one hundred acres each, under the royal order of 1790." He has not proved compliance with the conditions, and the claim is rejected.

* Claimant subsequently filed his petition for this land under the Donation Act, which was rejected. Vide No. 23, of Report 2, on Donation Claims.

No. 76.

WILLIAM CAIN, *Claimant—200 acres of land.*

This is a British grant, made to John Burnett, by Governor Moultrie, and sold to Cain on the 10th March, 1781. The lands lie on the South fork of Nassau river. In the memorial to this Board, the representatives of Cain call themselves citizens of the United States, and residents of Florida. There is no evidence before this Board, that Cain took the oath of allegiance to the Spanish King, or that this claim was even recognized as valid by the Government here. It is therefore rejected.

No. 77.

GEORGE COPELAND, *Claimant—400 acres of land.*

To the petition of Henry B. Martin, under whom Copeland claims, on the 3d September, 1803, for 400 acres of land, in the Territory of Mosquitoe, Governor White decrees as usual, "That he shall have the number of acres that correspond to his laborers, which shall afterwards be surveyed to him on the express condition, that he take possession of the land within six months from the date of the decree." There is a deed filed in this office, executed by Martin in the year 1808, in the city of New York, to George Copeland, in which Martin calls himself "a resident of that city." There is no proof of possession within the six months, of a survey, or of subsequent cultivation, on the part of Martin, and this deed describing himself as a citizen of New York, five years after the concession, is positive proof of abandonment.

No. 78.

JAMES DARLEY, *Claimant—500 acres of land.*

This land lies at Mosquito. There is no evidence of title filed before this Board, but the survey of Robert McHardy, dated 25th January, 1818. In his memorial to the Board, he has referred to documents filed in the claim immediately following this, as evidence of a grant made to him by Governor Coppinger in the preceding year.

No. 79.

JAMES DARLEY, *Claimant—500 acres of land.*

This land lies on Turnbull's swamp. It appears by the certificate of Thomas Aguilar, the original of which is not to be found, that on the application of the claimant, one thousand acres of land were granted him by Governor Coppinger, as head rights, on the 14th June, 1817; one half of which, No. 78, of this abstract, was surveyed to him at Mosquito, and the other half in Turnbull's swamp, on the 20th June, 1818. He has produced no evidence to prove his cultivation, or to account for the loss of the original. Both of these claims are, therefore, rejected.

No. 80.

PAUL DUPON, *Claimant—3000 acres of land.*

Paul Dupon solicited from the Government, (and there was granted to him, on the 8th May, 1818,) a small island situated on the East side of the river St. Johns, bounded on the South and East, by a creek, called Dunn's creek, which island contains 3000 acres; and on the 26th April, 1819, Governor Coppinger issued to said Dupon, a royal title for the above mentioned island, under the royal order of 1790. This claim is barred by the treaty.

No. 81.

JAMES MUNROE, *Claimant—2000 acres of land.*

James Munroe states to the Governor, "that, previous to his removing into the Province of East Florida, he authorized Alexander Drysdale to petition to the said Government on his behalf for lands, for head rights, having at that time forty negroes; but through a mistake, Drysdale only mentions four negroes, therefore the Government only granted 300 acres at Mosquito to Monroe." On the 3d August, 1803, Munroe petitioned the Government for the remaining quantity added to the 300 acres already granted, having brought into the province fifty negroes. To which Governor White made the following decree, on the same day, month, and year:

"Let there be granted to this party, the residue of the land which he solicits, up to the quantity which he is entitled to, for the 50 negroes belonging to him, without injury to a third person, and with the condition, that he must take possession of said land, in the term of six months, counted from this date."

F. BETHUNE.

The only witness sworn in the case, deposes that Munroe lived on the land four or five* left it. We consider that an abandonment before the ten years occupancy, forfeited the land. It is rejected.

AUGUSTINE BUYCK, *Claimant.*

No 82. 1,500 *acres land,*
No. 83. 1,500 *do.*
No. 84. 2,000 *do.*
No. 85. 50,000 *do.*

No. 82.

John De Pierra's certificate, the only document of title, is to this effect: "That to the memorial of Augustine Buyck, praying for 1,500 acres of land in the vicinity of the old town of St. Peters, at Mosquitoe, in the place called Spruce pear Creek, otherwise Haile's Creek, the following decree was rendered: 'The lands solicited by the petitioner are granted, and until,

*Here is an omission in the original.

according to the number of his family, the corresponding quantity of land be measured for him." The certificate and decree are both dated on the 18th day of July, 1801. The party, in his memorial to this Board, declares that the land had been surveyed.

No. 83.—2,000.

On the very same day and year, John De Pierra certifies, that, on the petition of Buyck, *praying for* 1,500 *acres of land in the vicinity of the old town of St. Peters, at Mosquitoe*, in a swamp or hammock situated opposite to Mount Oswald, towards the beach or North of the town, Gov. White decreed: "The lands solicited by Augustine Buyck are granted, &c. and until, &c." The original of this last grant is not on file in the Office of the Archives. This last, if not a forgery, is evidently a grant for the same land as in No. 82. Gov. White never granted two tracts of land on the same day, to the same individual, without taking notice, in either, of that fact: and it is a fraud on the part of Buyck, or his agent, to attempt thus to impose them on the Board, as several.

No. 84.—2,000 *acres.*

A grant by concession, in 1799, of two thousand acres of land "to the South of the town of Matanzas, and until. &c." Buyck's name does not appear on the list of lands surveyed by Marrot, in 1801. It is plain, then, that, at that time, he had not settled them, or that he failed to survey them, which we consider equally fatal. The memorial to the Board avows that they never were surveyed.

No. 85.—50,000.

The memorial of this party to the Governor, in 1802, and his memorial to this Board in 1823, present a curious contrast. In 1802, he says to the Governor: "That, possessing an increased number of new negroes, and some white natives of America desiring to associate with him, &c. he solicits 50,000 acres of land at Musquitoe," not wishing to exclude Ambrose Hull, who, *though then*, driven *away* by the Indians, is determined to return *as soon as an increased number of settlers* shall afford him protection; but adds, "that no obstacle should be allowed to prevent the grant to him, because grants of the same kind had been made to others—they "having spent so much time, without taking any steps towards the cultivation pretended, *any right they may have had, is lost.*" The petitioner promises peremptorily, "to make good the said establishment, between this (22d July, 1802,) and the month of next December; which time being past, it will remain at your Excellency's discretion to grant that territory to whoever may ask for it." He goes on to add: "a considerable number of planters, whom the subscriber offers to bring to that place, will have a sufficient field-force to fulfil the royal intentions, *and restrain the rapacity of the savages*, who have, up to this time, infested the plantations established to the North (quere South?) of this city."

The lands are granted on the condition, "that he cannot cede them away, without permission."

In his petition for the land, he gives as an inducement to the grant, a pledge to repress the Indians. In a memorial to us, he gives as a reason for not cultivating the lands, the hostility of these Indians, to suppress whom, he had pledged himself. It is too absurd for argument.

The claimant has tendered a receipt for 30 dollars paid by him, as a tax on his property in 1803. This is the first time we have learned that Spanish planters were assessed in taxes.

Charles W. Clarke swears that Buych settled here in 1792, and was driven off by the savages in 1800. It appears in Buych's petition for land, No. 84, that he had lived at another place, as he there declares that he had sold or commuted some other lands, of which he speaks.

If the evidence is intended to apply to either of these cases, Mr. Clarke is mistaken. The first grant is made in 1799; but the testimony of Mr. Clarke is perfectly correct, as explained by the party's memorial in the case alluded to. These cases are therefore rejected, because the party does not prove continued possession, nor can the hostility of the savages be received as an excuse, when the largest grant made, if made at all, was induced by the promise of Buych to suppress them. We will add, that there is no evidence that the grant of 50,000 acres was ever in the office of Archives; and that Governor White was not in the habit of making large grants on slight causes.

No. 86.

Buych and Dupont, *Claimants—small Island of land.*

Buyck and Dupont asked leave "to make lime and build a hut, on a small Island, between the two bars of the river Mantanzas."

The Governor, Quesada, in 1794, granted the leave asked, and adds, "but not to be considered their property until the general survey takes place, when it may, or may not, be included in their complement, if it is fit, proper, or not." We follow the translation, though it seems a bad one. It does not appear that any subsequent steps was taken in this business and on this permission to make lime, with an express declaration that the property is not granted. Buyck claims the land. Such are many of the claims in this office. It is rejected.

Jame McGirt, *Claimant.*

No. 87.——*acres land.*
No. 88. 500 *do.*
No. 89. 300 *do.*
No. 90. *small Island of* 90 *acres.*
No. 91. 500 *acres pine land.*
No. 92.——*land.*
No. 93. 600 *acres land.*

No. 94.

D. McGirt, the Son.

In 1796, an application to take the plantation of the widow Ashley, then vacant, in exchange for those which had been granted to him in 1794, which he had been compelled to abandon. Decree, "that he might take possession, until the survey was made and his portion allotted to him."

No. 88.—500 *acres.*

An application in 1792, from McGirt, who stiles himself an old inhabitant, for several tracts, viz: 300 acres, nine miles from this place, on a plantation which formerly belonged to Governor Grant,

200 acres on Suwannce Creek, near the other, and

300 acres on Nassau River, for cattle raising.

The Governor, Quesada, directs Marrot to survey to the applicant, the lands asked for.

No. 89.—300 *acres.*

Another petition for 300 acres of land, on Bells' Creek, on the St. Mary's, "as a part of the land which appertains to him." This is in 1793. Quesada directed Marrot to report, "whether any lands had been surveyed to Mc Girt, and on the propriety of the present application specially."

Marrot states in his report, the grants made in 1792, as specified above in No. 88. which lands had not been surveyed, and adds, "that in March, of the same year, he, McGirt, was permitted to abandon the 300 acres on Governor Grant, and to take, in its place, 300 acres on Black Creek, which John McQueen had surveyed to him." Marrot reported that "the place asked for is vacant, and that the petitioner is an old inhabitant;" and Quesada directed "always according to the number of the family which the party may have, &c. let there be measured, &c."

No. 90.—*An Island of* 80 *acres.*

The petitioner states that he had by permission, moved to St. Mary's, where he had not land enough, and solicits the grant of a little Island of 80 acres, opposite his plantation, which had been once ceded to Thomas Criar: who had abandoned it. He asks a further grant of a piece of land on the lower part of the Rose's Bluff, "which is convenient for the cutting of materials for building the houses he shall have to erect." This is in 1798.

The Engineer says, there is no objection to the grant of the land first asked for; but "that the grant to cut lumber, should be limited to the quantity wanted for his buildings." Thus it appears, that Rose's Bluff was not intended to be conveyed away; such in every case of mill grants is the decree, viz: "That he cut timber," and yet in those cases, the land is now claimed.

The Governor directs the land to be granted, "until his portion should be allotted," and that "the permission to cut timber, should be limited as advised by the Engineer."

No. 91.

500 *acres pine land.*

In 1799, McGirt represented to Governor White, that he had no pine land attached to his tract on St. Mary's, and prayed that 500 acres of pine land, the most convenient to his place, be granted.

Pierza makes a note, that this land was granted to John Lowe, in 1803.

No. 92.

—— *acres.*

A permit to John McQueen and James McGirt, to make the exchange alluded to in No. 89, and the parties claim it as a separate grant.

No. 93.

600 *acres.*

In January, 1792, Don Pedro Marrot certifies, "That he had measured to McGirt, 18 cavallerias, (600 acres of land) at a place called Andrew's Point, on account of what corresponds to him; whose family consists, according to the oath taken, of 14 persons, to wit: husband, wife, six children, and six negroes." This tract is situated on the River St. John's.

No. 94.

DANIEL McGIRT—*the Son.*

From what we can infer from the phraseology of this party's memorial to Governor White, in 1797, it seems that, as he was going to get married, he wanted permission from the Governor to take a piece of land on the River St. John's, called *Longs*, formerly granted to his father, James.

The Engineer, when it is referred to him, reported, that he could not find any grant of the lands in demand to his father, but advises that it be given to Daniel, in the usual manner, which is done.

James McGirt's name appears no where on the list of Marrot, except on that of 1801, where he is registered as possessing 680 acres of land, in his "statement of inhabitants on the Rivers Nassau and St. Mary's," and his son Daniel, for 200 acres on the same list.

It appears to the Board, from an examination of all these cases, that James McGirt was an old settler. The best evidence of the quantity to which he was entitled, is to be found in the certificate of Marrot, No. 93. By this it appears, that 600 acres were his just portion. These, by subsequent abandonments and exchanges, were finally located on St. Mary's, in a tract of 300 acres, No. 89, and 300 on Nassau, for cattle raising. The other 80 acres, which make up his compliment of 680 in the list of surveys by Marrot, is the island petitioned for in No. 90. We are willing to confirm this claim of James McGirt, and his heirs, to 680 acres of land, as surveyed by Marrot, viz: 300 acres on Nassau, No. 88; 300 acres on Bell's Creek, St. Mary's, No. 89; the island of 80, opposite thereto, No. 90.

McGirt states, that he was an old settler in 1792: he is so termed by Marrot; and in 1801, he is found on those tracts in the general survey.

The exchanges from place to place were, some by compulsion, and all by permission. It is fair to infer, that he lived out the term of ten years, and became entitled to the land.

The land granted to Daniel McGirt, in 1797, was on St. John's: in 1801, at the general survey, he is on the St. Mary's. He has not proved the duration of his possession, and it is rejected.

No. 95.

SARAH TATE, *Claimant*—450 *acres of land.*

These are the same lands confirmed to George Anderson. It will appear by reference to the printed reports of the Land Commissioners of East Florida, that the claimant's ancestor, Edward Tate, in 1811, represented to the Governor, that he had been employed so long at Picolata, that he had lost his buildings erected at Tomoca, on this land, granted in 1803, and that they, the Tomoca lands, were granted to Sans as vacant lands. He therefore prays his Excellency to grant him, in place thereof, 450 acres of land on the River St. Johns. This grant on the St. John's was made accordingingly, and confirmed to claimant on the 22d January, 1824, and now the Tates claim both. It is absurd: this claim is rejected.

No. 96.

JOHN B. GAUDRY, *claimant—3000 acres of land.*

On the 6th of October, 1817, the claimant, by his attorney, B. de Castro y Ferrer, petitioned for 3000 acres at Spring Garden, having a family and seventy-five negro slaves. The Governor granted the land on the 8th, with the proviso "that, as soon as he should make it appear that he is in possession, and cultivates it without intermission, the title of property shall be issued to him, agreeably to the survey and plat, which the surveyor shall present. Two months afterwards, it was surveyed by McHardy. Seven months from the date of the concession, the claimant, by his attorney, again represented to the Governor that he had performed the conditions, and petitioned for a full title.

He tenders several witnesses to prove the occupation and cultivation, with which the Governor seems perfectly satisfied, as, by his decree of the 14th of the same month, he pronounces it proved "that claimant had complied with the conditions imposed on him," and directs "that, in virtue of the royal order, granting lands to new settlers, a full title shall be executed to him, according to the plat and survey."

We have frequently decided that, where the date of the concession would admit the presumption that the party had lived out his ten years on the land, a royal title, or any other act done by the Governor, though subsequent to the 24th of January, 1818, would be received by this Board as conclusive proof to show that the claimant had performed the conditions, and cultivated the land; but, when the concession is dated in October, it is mere mockery, in the subsequent May, to talk of continued cultivation. On the first organization of the Board of Commissioners, in 1823, the claimant, in his memorial, represented himself as "a resident of Georgia;" it is evident, then, that, in 1822 or 23, he had abandoned the land, and, as the Governor's power to make grants on the 24th January, 1818, was ended by the treaty, this claim rests upon the concession alone, and, although the Governor was satisfied with the proof before him, it convinces us that the claimant lived but a few months on the land, and he therefore must lose it.

No. 97.

PETER MITCHELL, *claimant—550 acres of land.*

The memorial of P. Mitchell to this Board, states that, in 1813, this tract of land was granted in absolute property to John McClure, by Governor Kinderlan, and that the royal title, together with the survey made by John Purcell, in 1811, are on file in the office of Public Archives of this city."

He further states, that this tract of land, on the demise of J. McClure, was, by his legal representatives, conveyed to George Atkinson, in trust for the house of Carnookau & Mitchell, of which Peter Mitchell is a partner.

There are but two documents filed in this case. The certificate of George F. Clarke, to which we shall presently refer, and the survey made by Peter Mitchell himself, in 1823, of 550 acres of land on the river Ocklewaha. If there was a royal title to McClure, it has not been brought to this office. It seems, from the certificate of Clarke, above alluded to, that the title of McClure, in the wording, embraced the whole of the land on which stood the fortifications, town, and commons of Fernandina." Clarke says, in 1813, when, by the commission of the Government, he, Clarke, was engineer of the fortifications, and distributor of the town lots of that place, McClure stopped his progress by exhibiting his title to the soil. On this, Clarke wrote to Gov Kinderlan, and received the following answer:

"I am surprised that Don John McClure should have stopped you in the measurement of lots, which has been committed to your charge by Government. He never could have supposed that the title given him could be *in* injury to the lands that were previously destined for the habitations of those who settled in the town of Fernandina. Therefore, you will warn him, by my order, to desist from embarrassing, in any wise, your functions therein; and inform him that, if he has any thing to allege in support of his right, before a competent tribunal, that is, in case he has sustained injury by the establishment of said settlement, on *these* being made manifest, he will be compensated by an equal quantity of land, in a convenient place, without injury to a third person."

Clarke further certifies, "that, sometime after this, John McClure having died, his cousin, another John McClure, came to Florida, and obtained an order for the sale of all the property of the deceased; this tract was advertised amongst the rest of the deceased's property. Clarke forbade the sale, and the commandant of that place, having failed to interpose, when required so to do by Clarke, the Governor, Coppinger, was again applied to; this is in March, 1816; in April of the same year, Coppinger writes the following letter to the civil and military commandant of that place, with a copy of which, Clarke was furnished. "Having been informed on the 28th of last month, by Don George Clarke, Surveyor &c. at Fernandina, respecting the sale of McClure's plantation, &c. I require, that you comply exactly with the order of the 19th July, 1813, passed to the aforesaid surveyor by my predecessor, permitting the sale to take place, only as to those lands that are not wanted, nor comprehended in the settlement and fortifications thereof, and make known to the person interested, that he is to direct his recourse to this Government, who will compensate him for the land of which he is dismembered, with an equal portion in any vacant place, that may suit him, without injury to a third person."

Clarke further certifies, "that, in 1821, F. Bethune, on the part of the claimants, petitioned the Governor for 550 acres of land in "compensation" of the defalcation of said tract of land, which part he abandons, with all his rights, for the public good of said town."

To this memorial, Coppinger answers in a private letter to Clarke, "that he was officially informed of the transfer of the province to the United States, and could not make the grant."

Clarke says, that this quantity of 550 acres was rather more in amount than McClure had lost, but from his knowledge of the sentiments on this subject

subject of both the Governors, Kinderlan and Coppinger, he is fully confident that it would have been granted, if applied for in time, without hesitation; and he says further, that if he had been called on, as surveyor general, by the representatives of John McClure, "to survey to him this amount for the further approbation and formalization of the same by Government, he would have done so, as he more than once offered to do." From this it appears evident that the parties were entitled to some land, as McClure's representatives, from the Spanish Government, but they have neglected to avail themselves of their privilege, until it was too late; and if Governor Coppinger, in 1821, thought that he had no power to make the grant, in 1823 Peter Mitchell had no power to make the location. It is rejected.

No. 98.

Hibberson and Yonge, *Claimants—45 acres of land.*

This is Aguilar's certificate, that, on the 25th January, 1810, the Governor granted this land, near the military post of Amelia Island, and authorized John Purcell to survey it. It does not appear that it was surveyed, nor is there proof of cultivation. It is rejected.

No. 99.

Robert Hutchinson, *Claimant—150 acres of land on Little St. Mary's Swamp.*

This claim is for 150 acres: in support of it, he presents a certificate of Aguilar, that, on the 13th February, 1816, 450 acres were granted him as head rights.

There is no evidence of cultivation, and no reason given for the loss of the original. It is rejected.

No. 100.

Samuel King, *Claimant—300 acres of land.*

This land lies on the south side of the river Nassau, about 10 miles from its mouth. In 1804, the application was made to Governor White, "on account of the death of Margaret Carter, who claimed said land, as belonging to her deceased husband, James Sample." The Governor directed him to hold possession of the land, 300 acres, and the concession to be considered as in force from the 9th March, 1803. This grant is made under the royal order of 1790; and, no cultivation being proved, it is rejected.

No. 101.

The widow and heirs of Antonio Martinez, *Claimants—70 acres of land, on Moultrie creek.*

This grant was made on the 3d June, 1806, by concession from Gov. White, and was surveyed by James Purcell in the following July. It is for "head rights" without proof of cultivation. Rejected.

No. 102.

Rob. Pritchard's Heirs, *Claimants—700 acres of land—at Goldsby's Lake.*

This is Aguilar's certificate, dated in the year 1800. White decreed that the land should be granted "until, according to the number of persons he may have for its cultivation, there be allotted him that which he is entitled to."

It will be seen by reference to No. 21 of report A, that, in 1808, upon a full hearing of the whole matter, Gov. White directed 270 acres to be granted to the widow of R. Pritchard, "that being the whole amount to which, from the number of her family, black and white, she was entitled." That amount has been confirmed to her.

This tract of land was surveyed by Geo. Clarke in 1819; and three witnesses swear that the claimant lived on the South side of Goldsby's Lake, on a tract said to contain 700 acres. The 270 acres confirmed are at the same place, on the South side of Goldsby's Lake, and on this the Claimants have resided. Gov. White thought them entitled to 270 acres of land only; and this claim is rejected.

No. 103.

Gachalan Vass, *Claimant—250 acres of land—Pablo Creek.*

In 1793, this land was surveyed by Marrot; he does not prove possession for the ten years required. And it is rejected.

No. 104.

James Tool, *Claimant—945 acres of land—in Graham's Swamp.*

A permission in 1803, by Gov. White, to have the lands which correspond to him; no further steps seem to have been taken in the case. No proof of his family, of survey, or of cultivation. It is rejected.

No. 105.

Francis Triay, *Claimant— acres land on the North River.*

A concession in the usual form in 1802, without proof of cultivation. Rejected.

No. 106.

William Travers, *Claimant—100 acres of land on Potsburg Creek.*

Concession in 1799 to John McQueen, without proof of cultivation. Rejected.

No. 107.

ISAAC TUCKER, *Claimant—200 acres of land.*

This is Aguilar's certificate. "That in 1804 the claimant petitioned for 200 acres of land, and Gov. White gave him but 100 acres, declaring that to be all to which he was entitled." The grant, if made at all, lies on the River St. Mary's. In 1817, Geo. Clarke surveyed this land, on the River St. John's, at a place called ———, 2 miles below the Cowford; and, in 1821, Geo. Clarke changed the location to another point upon the same river. There is no proof of cultivation, and we cannot confirm it.

No. 108.

GABRIEL TRIAY, *Claimant—Key Vacas.*

Concession dated 2d January, 1818, for military services. The title of the United States to this Key was relinquished by the Board of Land Commissioners to some other claimant.

No. 109.

FARQUHAR BETHUNE, *Claimant—172 acres of land.*

This land is situated on Amelia Island, near the lands of Thomas Yonge, on Egan's Creek.

The evidence of title is a concession made by Estrada, on the 25th August, 1815, under the order of 1790. The application of Bethune is for 100 acres of land, and this is the quantity ceded; but Geo. J. F. Clarke, on the 13th December, 1818, in the plenitude of his power, surveyed to Bethune 172 acres. Clarke, produced as a witness before the board, has deposed, that Bethune did cultivate the land during the time that it was considered his property.

It appears from this affidavit, and the survey of Clarke already spoken of, that the one hundred acres on Amelia Island, had been taken from Bethune by the Government, and the survey of Clarke was made on St. Mary's River in lieu thereof. Clarke's survey then is too late, and the claim is rejected.

No. 110.

THOMAS BACKHOUSE, *Claimant—500 acres of land—on Indian River.*

A grant by Royal Title, made on the 20th June, 1818, for services. Rejected. We believe this to be the same claim as No. 4 of this report.

No. 111.

WM. H. G. SAUNDERS, *Claimant—1200 acres of land—St. Johns River.*

On the 10th September, 1791, Gov. Quesada made to John Saunders, ancestor of the Claimant, a concession for the land in question.

This is one of the first grants made under the order of 1790; and differs materially in its phraseology, from the abbreviated concessions, subsequently adopted. It commences in the usual form, and follows the formalities of a royal title. It grants and concedes the land in perpetuity, and then attaches the following conditions: "That Saunders shall, within two years, build a house proportioned to his means; that he shall clean and clear the land, for the purpose of cultivating; and that he shall have, within the term of three years, at least five head of horned cattle, for every fifty acres of land not fit for cultivation," &c. "and, finally, although this donation and concession is made in perpetuity, the donee or his heirs cannot alienate or transfer the said lands to any other owner, until the ten years of possession be passed; and, even then, the first sale must be executed with permission of the Government, and, in any other way, it should be null," &c.

The Governor proceeds to say, "Under the said conditions, and not without them, I cede, renounce, and transfer the said land," &c. Mary Carney, the witness produced on the part of the claimant, deposes, that John Saunders, the grantee, in the years 1790 and 1791, with his family, and a pretty large number of negroes, lived on the land claimed, built houses thereon, and made one crop; and that, in 1791, he was compelled to leave it, in consequence of the disturbances upon the river. On the 11th September, 1792, we hear from Saunders again. In a memorial to the Governor, he then represented the place, called Russellton, the one now claimed, "as very noxious to the health, as well from the greater part being infested by corrupted vapours, which are exhaled from the putrid waters of the swamps and lakes, which surround it, as also from the many insects engendered in the marshes," &c. He says, moreover, that "the health of his family is deteriorated, their bodies oppressed and troubled with swellings, and threatened with dropsy." Wherefore he prays "the benignant heart of the Governor, condoling with his deplorable state, to grant him, in exchange, an equal quantity of land on Mosquitoe." The Governor, on the reception of Captain Marrot's report, "that the land at Russellton is surrounded by putrid waters," directed Marrot to survey to him an equal quantity, at the place solicited. In 1796, Saunders, for mal-practices against the Government, was banished the province; and, a few years afterwards, as we believe, the most of this tract was granted to another, as vacant land. Since the change of flags, the present claimant, the son of John, has moved into the Territory, and taken possession of the place.

Such is the history of this case: so far as these lands have been re-granted, the parties litigant have their remedy at law; so far as they have not, the claim of Saunders is rejected: First, because the title under which he claims, is a bare concession to his father, with conditions attached, which were never performed; for, although the houses were completed, nothing else was done: Secondly, because the party himself solicited an exchange, which was granted him: Thirdly, because he was banished, and his lands thereby forfeited; and, Fourthly, because, by the testimony of his own witness, he lived but one year upon the land; and, if there had been no exchange, no mal-practice, and no banishment, this would be insufficient to justify us in confirming this claim.

No. 112.

WILLIAM TRAVERS, AGENT OF YELLOWLY, *Claimant*—*500 acres of land.*

No. 113.

William Dry, *Claimant*—1,000 *acres of land.*

No. 114.

Same—a lot in St. Augustine.

No. 115.

Same—a lot in St. Augustine.

These are all British claims, which seem not to have been recognized by the Spanish Government; and must be rejected.

No. 112 was granted by Governor Tonyn, in April, 1777. It lies in Derbin's Swamp, three-fourths of a mile East of the River St. Johns.

No. 113 was granted to Alexander Gray, by James Grant, in February, 1771. It lies on the East fork of Diego River, and was sold by Gray to the present claimant, in 1775.

The other two are for lots in this City, claimed by Dry, a British subject. They are all rejected.

No. 116.

Andrew Atkinson, *Claimant*—100 *acres of land.*

This land is claimed by concession, dated in February, 1792, "as necessary to complete the number of acres belonging to his family." It lies near St. Vincent Ferrer. There is no evidence of cultivation, and it must be rejected.

No. 117.

The Heirs of Antonio Andrew, *Claimants*—500 *acres of land.*

In 1796 these lands were granted under the royal order of 1790. There is no number of acres specified in the memorial of the party, or in the decree of the Governor. The lands lie at New Smyrna.

Two witnesses have been sworn. George Clarke says, that they, the claimants, were a number of years settled on the land, and were driven off about 30 years ago by the Indians. Lorenzo Capella, the other witness, seems to be more minutely informed on the subject. He says the claimants were settled on the land, and made one crop, and were ready to make a second, when the Indians forced them to abandon it. These depositions were taken in the year 1827; thirty years ago will bring us back to 1797. The concession was made in 1796, one year before. This proves, conclusively, that Mr. Clarke was mistaken, in supposing the family had lived on the land a number of years, and that Capella is correct in saying, that they left it after one year.

This Board has always decided, that one year's cultivation, whatever might be the cause of abandonment, would not justify us in confirming a claim. It is rejected.

No. 118.

John Jones, *Claimant—500 acres of land.*

The concession under the royal order of 1790, "until the quantity to which he is entitled shall be surveyed to him," is dated on the 11th February, 1801. Marrot's list of the inhabitants on St. John's, of 27th February, 1801, does not contain his name. There is no evidence of cultivation, and it is rejected. One hundred acres have been already confirmed to John Jones, report (No. 4 and No. 31) of 1828, this session; and we imagine this to be the same person, and all the land to which he is entitled.

No. 119.

Ezekiel Tucker, *Claimant—150 acres of land.*

This land lies on the river Nassau, at a place called Tucker's Creek. It was granted by Governor Coppinger by concession, dated 18th March, 1817, under the order of 1790.

The claimant has produced no evidence of cultivation, and it is rejected.

No. 120.

Stephen Eubank, *Claimant—255 acres of land.*

There is a concession for this land, signed by Governor White, and dated on the 4th February, 1806. The only description of the land in the paper presented to us is, "That it is bounded on the East by lands granted to E. Tucker."

The concession of White required, that the party should establish himself on the land within one month. There is no proof that he did so, or that he possessed it subsequently. It is rejected.

No. 121.

Paul Dupon, *Claimant—3000 acres of land.*

This land lies at Spring Garden. The basis of the claim is this: A concession from Governor Coppinger, dated 8th October, 1817, in virtue of the royal order of 1790; a certificate of survey, the 8th December, 1817; a memorial for an absolute title, dated 9th May, 1819; and a decree for taking testimony to prove settlement and cultivation, together with the testimony of Robert McHardy, A. Burgevin, and Fr. Ferreitra, of the same date. Then follows the decree of the Governor, for an absolute title, and the title itself made on the same day, the 14th May, 1818.

It will appear by reference to No. 80, of this report, that the Governor, about this time, had granted another tract of the same quantity to the same individual.

This claim is almost precisely similar to that of Jno. B. Gaudry, reported No. 96, above, and for the reasons given there, to which we refer, it is rejected.

No. 122.

M. Villalonga, *Claimant—10 acres of land.*

No. 123.

Same—6 acres of land.

Thomas Aguilar certifies, that, on a favorable report of the commandant of engineers, Governor White, on the 24th October, 1801, granted 10 acres of land to the claimant, without the gates of St. Augustine, and within the 1500 yards, on the usual conditions.

No. 123 is also a certificate of Aguilar, that, on the 10th November, 1790, Quesada granted to the claimant 3 acres of land, which he possessed during the British dominion, "at a place called Marcazaz;" and on the 24th November, 1804, Governor White granted to the same individual, three acres more, at the same place.

As there is nothing in these cases but the certificate of Aguilar, we cannot confirm them.

No. 124.

Pablo F. Fontaine, *Claimant—3000 acres of land.*

This land is situated on Vackasasa creek, about ten leagues Southwest of Alachua. It purports to have been granted for military services, on the 15th May, 1815. This paper is not filed in the office of the archives, where it should certainly have been found, if the claim is genuine. The paper presented to us, is claimed to be the original, and proof of the signature of Kinderlan was tendered to this Board, but not received.

We have rejected this claim because we do not think it genuine, and for the following reasons:

The first is, that the land did lie within the Indian boundary; within which, grants were seldom made by the Spanish Governors.

Secondly, it is a well known fact, that little at that time was known of the country so much removed from the sea coast as this.

Thirdly, and above all, the grant is dated on the 15th May, 1815, by authority of a royal order of 29th March preceding, which was transmitted from Madrid, by way of Havana, and communicated to the Governor of this place, by the Captain General Apodaca, by a letter bearing date on the 7th July, 1815, nearly two months after the date of the grant.

No. 125.

Jacob Worldly, *Claimant—undefined acres of land.*

There is no evidence of title in this case. In November, 1806, Worldly makes an application to Governor White, to grant him on Trout creek the number of acres which might correspond to him and his family. Governor White, in the same month, directed Wm. Lawrence to report, whether or not Wordly possessed and cultivated the lands which he claimed. One year afterwards Lawrence made a favorable report of this fact, and here the matter seems to have rested. As there is no proof in the office to show that any subsequent steps were taken, to consummate the title, and as this claim was filed here on the 12th November, 1826, it is rejected.

No. 126.

EZEKIEL TUCKER, *Claimant*—100 *acres of land.*

In 1805, Tucker, representing himself as an American citizen, applied to Governor White for 200 acres of land, about 65 miles North of this city, and 20 South of St Mary's, at a place called Nassau. Governor White directed that 100 acres should be granted, on this condition, amongst others, "That he should establish himself upon it, within the term of six months." There is no proof that he did so then, or at any subsequent period; and we doubt whether Governor White would have granted land to an American citizen in the face of a royal order, which forbid it. This, too, as well as No. 125, was filed in this office, on the 12th November last; and, for all of these reasons, either of which would be amply sufficient, it is rejected.

No. 127.

PEDRO PESO DE BURGO, *Claimant*—400 *acres of land.*

The grant to this land is dated 15th April, 1815; it is therefore bad. It was made for military services, and is situated at St. Vincent Ferrer, on the river St. Johns. Rejected.

No 128.

HANNAH SMITH, *Claimant*—400 *acres of land.*

In 1817, the claimant applied to Governor Coppinger for 400 acres, on Deep creek, under the order of 1790, and they were conceded.

It does not appear that the claimant has ever cultivated the land. James Hall, in whose veracity, as it will appear by our report of the last session, we place no confidence, has sworn, generally, that the state of the country was such, at the date of the concession, as to make it dangerous to locate a settlement, but it does not appear that, since the change of flags, Mrs. Smith has made the attempt, as, by the provisions of the treaty with Spain, it was her duty to do; it is therefore rejected.

No. 129.

CHARLES GOBERT, *Claimant*—2000 *acres of Land.*

In November, 1804, Charles Gobert presented a memorial to Governor White, in which he avowed his determination to cultivate coffee in the Province, and applied for 2000 acres of land, situated on Dunn's Island, about ten miles South of a place called Rallstown, East side of St. Johns river, in lieu of 2000 acres theretofore granted him at Mosquitoe. The decree of the Governor is, that the land shall be granted, with the same conditions under which Drayton's Island was granted to Geo. Sibbald, "specifying said conditions in the certificate, which shall be issued to him from the Secretary's coffie.

This claim should be rejected for uncertainty; the certificate spoken of should have been produced, and this uncertainty would have been removed.

We have examined the grant of Drayton's Island to Sibbald, which was acted on by the Board of Land Commissioners, and find their decree to be in the following words: "the Board having ascertained that this claim is covered by a British grant, they therefore order that it be reported to Congress for their determination." From this decree it was impossible for us to ascertain the nature of the grant to Sibbald; we have, therefore, deemed it our duty to look into the grant itself. The original concession, specifying the particular conditions, is not before us. But the Royal title made to Kingsley, the purchaser from Sibbald, in 1815, presents the following facts in the case: first, that the land was granted to George Sibbald, in 1804, under the Royal order of 1790: secondly, that the lands were adjudged to Kinsley, by a decree of the Government, in 1811; and thirdly, in the language of the instrument of the title, "considering that he has already passed more than ten years of uninterrupted possession to obtain the useful and direct dominion of the said Island of Drayton, made buildings on it cultivated it, and finally complied with all the other conditions established by the Government for grants and concessions of this nature," the Royal title aforesaid, was granted him. From all this, it appears that these lands were granted under the order of 1790, which required ten years' peaceable possession to make a concession valid. In the case of Drayton's Island, this continued possession was proved to Kindelan, and he has given a valid title. In the case before us, nothing has been proved, and the title is bad. Independent of this, we believe this to be the same land subsequently granted to Thomas Murphy, No. 41 of this report, and if it be so, the Spanish Government must have considered that, in 1818, Gobert had failed to comply with the conditions imposed, and that this land was public property. Rejected.

No. 130.

JOSEPH M. HERNANDEZ, *Claimant—A marsh lot (undefined.)*

On the 8th April, 1818, Governor Coppinger gave to the claimant a Royal title to the marsh in front of his plantation.

No. 131.

SEBASTIAN GARCIA, *Claimant—15 acres Land.*

No. 132.

SAME *Claimant—6 acres.*

These two claims are situated outside of the city of St. Augustine: No. 131, at a place called Aigachy, near Mose, and No. 132, without the new lines of the city, adjoining the lands of John Gianopoly. No. 131 is a concession from Governor Quesada, of the 9th of Nov. 1792. No. 132 was conceded by Governor White, in 1802. There is no evidence of cultivation in either case, and they are both rejected.

CHARLES DOWNING, *Register.*
WILLIAM H. ALLEN, *Receiver.*

REPORT No. 2.

REGISTER of Claims to Land which have been rejected by the

Numbers.	NAMES OF PRESENT CLAIMANTS.	NAMES OF ORIGINAL CLAIMANTS.	Date of Patent or Royal Title.	Date of Concession, or order of Survey.	Quantity of Land. Acres. hdths.
1	Bartholomew Sauraz -	Bartholomew Sauraz	Aug. 4, 1818	- -	50.00
2	Pablo Sabati - -	Pablo Sabati -	April 2, 1818	- -	2,500.00
3	Estevan Arnau - -	Estevan Arnau -	June 19, 1818	- -	100.00
4	Thomas Backhouse -	Thomas Backhouse	June 20, 1818	- -	500.00
5	Moses E. Levy -	Joaquin Sanchez -	June 15, 1818	- -	500.00
6	John Houston - -	John Houston -	- -	May 20, 1818	700.00
7	John Gonzalez - -	John Gonzalez -	June 19, 1818	- -	1,000.00
8	Fr. D. McDonell -	F. D. McDonell -	- -	- -	800.00
9	Octavious Mitchell -	Octavious Mitchell -	- -	June 2, 1818	2,000.00
10	William T. Hall -	William T. Hall -	- -	Oct. 20, 1819	2,000.00
11	Flora Leslie - -	Flora Leslie -	- -	April 12, 1810	500.00
12	Susannah Rollins -	Susanna Rollins -	- -	Dec. 6, 1799	200.00
13	Isabella Wiggins -	Isabella Wiggins -	- -	- -	300.00
14	J H McIntosh - -	John McQueen -	- -	Nov. 5, 1795	Undefined
15	Hannah Nobles - -	Robert Cowen -	- -	July 2, 1799	1,000.00
16	Thomas Saurez, administrator Antonio Saurez	Antonio Saurez -	- -	- -	500.00
17	Abner Williams' heirs -	Anastacio Mabrumaty	- -	June 2, 1801	150.00
18	Edward R Gibson -	Julian D. Suiny -	- -	July 1, 1815	125.00
19	George Morrison -	George Morrison -	- -	May 2, 1805	150.00
20	Charlotte Gobert -	Charles (free negro)	- -	Dec 4, 1806	100.00
21	Daniel Hurlburt -	Daniel Hurlburt -	- -	Sept. 3, 1805	125.00
22	Joseph Cone - -	Joseph Cone -	- -	May 29, 1805	115.00
23	Robert Hutchison -	Robert Hutchison -	- -	May 8, 1816	450.00
24	Heirs of Robert Andrew	Robert Andrew	- -	Oct. 18, 1793	100.00
25	Isabella Wiggins -	Isabella Wiggins -	- -	Aug. 6, 1815	300.00
26	Josiak Starkey's trustee	Charles F Sibbald	- -	- -	455.00
27	Joseph F White -	Alexander Watson -	- -	July 28, 1803	350.00
28	Robert Andrew -	R. Andrew -	- -	Nov. 18, 1779	100.00
29	Daniel C. Hart - -	Daniel C. Hart -	- -	Jan. 18, 1818	150.00
30	William Barden -	William Barden -	- -	May 6, 1805	50.00
31	James Lewis, Jun. -	James Lewis -	- -	Dec. 22, 1806	50.00
32	Widow of Ths. Collier -	Thomas Collier -	- -	May 8, 1804	1,200.00
33	Delia Broadaway -	Delia Broadaway -	- -	Sept. 15, 1815	500.00
34	Ant. Williams (free neg.)	Antonio Williams -	- -	Dec. 1, 1801	300.00
35	Albany Fallis - -	A Fallis - -	- -	Nov. 6, 1805	50.00
36	Michael Lynch - -	Michael Lynch -	- -	June 22, 1805	335.00
37	John G. Rushing -	John G Rushing -	- -	- -	80.00
38	Ezekiel Hudnall's heirs	Ezekiel Hudnall -	- -	June 3, 1817	900.00
39	Thomas Andrew -	Robert Andrew -	- -	Sept. 23, 1803	200.00
40	H, B. Martin - -	H B. Martin -	- -	Sept. 3, 1803	400.00
41	Thomas Murphey -	Thomas Murphey -	- -	June 11, 1818	3,000.00
42	William Hart - -	William Hart -	- -	June 11, 1811	1,400.00
43	Joseph B. Reyes -	Joseph B. Reyes -	- -	Sept. 15, 1803	1.700.00
44	Lewis Pike's heirs -	Lewis Pike -	- -	May 5, 1801	400.00
45	John Creighton -	John Creighton -	- -	Oct. 29, 1803	305.00
46	George Webber -	George Webber -	- -	Jan. 21, 1804	100.00
47	Thomas Yonge -	Isaac Wickes -	Mar. 31, 1818	July 23, 1803	1,100.00

REPORT No. 2.

Register and Receiver for the District of East Florida.

By whom conceded.	Authority or Royal Order under which the concession was granted.	Date of Survey.	By whom Surveyed.	WHERE SITUATED.
Coppinger	1815	-	-	Mose Creek.
Coppinger	1815	June 30, 1818	A. Burgevin -	East of Casacola.
Coppinger	1815	Oct. 20, 1818	R. McHardy -	Hillsborough River, Musquito.
Coppinger	1815	-	-	Indian River, south of St. Lucia.
Coppinger	1815	-	-	Jupiter Island, Indian River.
Coppinger	-	-	-	Dame's Point and Star Island, Nassau.
Coppinger	1790	June 28, 1819	A. Burgevin -	St. Diego.
Certificate *				
Coppinger	-	July 25, 1818	R. McHardy -	Musquito.
Coppinger	1815	July 24, 1818	Same -	Haul Over, Musquito.
White -	1790	-	-	Springer's Branch, 20 miles from St. Aug.
White -	1790	-	-	North Margin of a swamp, Nassau.
- -	-	Mar. 23, 1821	Go. J. F. Clarke	East side of Lake George.
Quesada -	1790	-	-	River Miami.
White -	1790	-	-	West side of Lake St. Marks.
- -	-	Mar. 1, 1817	G. J. F. Clarke	Mills' Swamp, Alligator Creek.
White -	1790	-	-	South side of River St. John.
Estrada -	1790	-	-	Head of Moultrie Creek.
White -	1790	-	-	St. Mary's River.
White -	1790	-	-	West side of St. Mark's Pond.
White -	1790	-	-	Pevet's Swamp.
White -	1790	-	-	St. Mary's River.
Coppinger	1790	-	-	Little St. Mary's River.
Quesada -	-	-	-	Savannas of Urtiche.
Coppinger	1790	-	-	East side of Lake George.
- -	-	July 8, 1816	G. J. F. Clarke	River St. Mary's.
White -	-	-	-	Graham's Swamp.
Quesada				
Coppinger	-	-	-	9 mile point of St. John's River.
White -	-	-	-	Pearson's Island, River Nassau.
- -	-	-	-	Quarter of a mile south of Buenavestor.
White -	-	-	-	Tomoco River.
- -	-	-	-	Dunn's Creek, St. Mary's River.
- -	-	-	-	St. Mark's Lagoon.
White -	-	-	-	On Nassau River.
- -	-	-	-	Between Halfax River and Tomoco Creek.
- -	-	Feb. 8, 1817	G. J. F. Clarke	North side of St. John's R. Chapbd. Cr.
Coppinger	-	April 1, 1821	Same -	East side of St. John's R. op. Dryton's Is.
White -	-	April 20, 1807	John Purcell -	Northwest side of St. John's River.
White				
- -	-	-	-	An Island on the St. John's River.
- -	-	-	-	River St. John's.
White -	1790	-	-	Three miles West of St. Augustine.
White -	1790	-	-	Twenty-seven miles North of St. Augus.
White -	1790	-	-	Pluni, St. John's River.
White -	1790	-	-	Graham's Creek.
Coppinger	1790	-	-	Besset's plantation, Musquitoe.

* A Certificate of Juan de Entralgo, of the 24th of May, 1819, that the claimant had no lands precedent to that date.

REPORT No. 2—Continued.

Numbers.	NAMES OF PRESENT CLAIMANTS.	NAMES OF ORIGINAL CLAIMANTS.	Date of Patent or Royal Title.	Date of Concession, or order of Survey.	Quantity of Land. Acres. hdths.
48	Heirs of Nath. Hall -	Nathaniel Hall -	- -	July 27, 1799	400.00
49	Elias B. Gould -	Geo. J. F. Clarke	- -	May 3, 1816	500.00
50	Heirs of A. Demilliere -	Augn. Demilliere -	- -	May 5, 1798	170.00
51	Francisco Paz - -	Francisco Paz -	- -	Nov. 12, 1815	1,500.00
52	James Dell - -	James Dell -	- -	Dec. 16, 1816	500.00
53	Heirs of John Faulk -	John Faulk -	- -	June 22, 1792	250.00
54	Frederick Hartley -	Frederick Hartley	- -	- -	400.00
55	Andrew Drouillard -	Andw. Drouillard -	- -	Jan. 10, 1818	3,000.00
56	William Hull - -	William Hull -	- -	Mar. 1, 1792	500.00
57	Joseph Mills - -	Joseph Mills -	- -	Feb. 15, 1793	200.00
58	William Ulmer -	William Ulmer -	- -	Sep. 15, 1803	200.00
59	David Turner - -	David Turner -	- -	Feb. 3, 1809	90.00
60	Pollard McCormock -	David McCormock	- -	July 13, 1803	2,000.00
61	William Ladd - -	William Ladd -	- -	Jan. 3, 1804	1,525.00
62	Hibberson & Yonge -	Hibberson & Yonge	- -	Feb. 23, 1815	2,000.00
63	James Pelot - -	James Pelot -	- -	- -	496.00
64	Same - -	James Pelot -	- -	- -	356.00
65	Josiah Dupont's heirs -	Josiah Dupont -	- -	1792	1,850.00
"	Same - -	Same -	- -	1794	500.00
"	Same - -	Same -	- -	July, 1801	500.00
"	Same - -	Gideon Dupont -	- -	May 27, 1802	1,400.00
66	Heirs of Philip Dill, (John H. McIntosh)	Philip Dill -	- -	1801	800.00
67	Clarissa Fish - -	Andrew Campbell	- -	1804	150.00
68	Francis Goodwin's heirs	Francis Goodwin -	- -	1791	1,300.00
				Feb'ry, 1792	1,300.00
69	John Love - -	John Love -	- -	1772	300.00
70	George Tillet - -	George Tillet -	- -	- -	250.00
71	Francis P. Sanchez -	John Perchman -	- -	1815	2,000.00
72	Hibberson & Yonge -	Hibberson & Yonge	- -	1815	2,000.00
73	John Bellamy - -	John Bellamy -	- -	- -	500.00
74	Susanna Cashen -	James Cashen -	- -	- -	300.00
75	John D. Kehr -	John D. Kehr -	- -	1801	300.00
76	William Cain - -	W. Cain (J. Burnett)	- -	- -	200.00
77	George Copeland -	H. B. Martin -	- -	1803	400.00
78	James Darley - -	James Darley -	- -	-	500.00
79	James Darley - -	James Darley -	- -	June 14, 1817	500.00
80	Paul Dupon - -	Paul Dupon -	April 26, 1819	May 8, 1818	3,000.00
81	James Munroe - -	James Munroe -	- -	August, 1803	2,000.00
82	Augustin Buyck -	Aug. Buyck -	- -	July 18, 1801	1,500.00
83	Same - -	Same -	- -	Same	1,500.00
84	Same - -	Same -	- -	1799	2,000.00
85	Same - -	Same -	- -	1802	50,000.00

REPORT No. 2—Continued.

By whom conceded.	Authority or Royal Order under which the concession was granted.	Date of Survey.	By whom Surveyed.	WHERE SITUATED
White -	1790	- -	- -	Banks of Trout Creek.*
- -	-	- -	- -	Big Bend, Durbin's Swamp.
White -	-	- -	- -	Rose's Bluff, St. Mary's River.
Estrada -	1815	- -	- -	Pellicer's Creek.
Coppinger	-	- -	- -	Hagin's Point, Alachua.
Quesada -	1790	- -	- -	Anderson's Cowpen, St. Mary's River.
- -	-	Mar 6, 1792	Pedro Marrot -	Nassau River.†
Coppinger	1790	April 15, 1818	Go. J. F. Clarke	North side of Dunn's Lake.
- -	-	- -	- -	River St. John's.
Quesada -	1790	- -	- -	Trout Creek.
White -	-	- -	-	Ten miles from New Smyrna.
White -	1790	- -	- -	North of St. John's R. head of Cedar Cr.
White -	1790	- -	- -	Penmann, Musquitoe.
White -	1790	- -	- -	Bissett's, Musquitoe.
Kindelan -	1815	Mar 21, 1816 June 24, 1821	G. J. F. Clarke	Trout Creek, and 12 mile Swamp.‡
- -	-	April 14, 1793	Pedro Marrot -	Pelot's Island, St. John's River.
- -	-	Mar. 31, 1793	Same -	Nassau River.
Quesada -	-	- -	- -	In the neighborhood of Mantanzas.
Same -	-	- -	- -	Same same.
White -	-	- -	- -	Graham's Swamp.
White	-	- -	- -	Graham's Swamp.
White -	-	- -	- -	River St. John's.
White -	-	-	- -	Mantanzas.
Quesada -	-	- -	- -	Pablo Creek.
Same -	-	- -	- -	St. Vincent Ferrier.
Tonyn -	-	- -	- -	Fifteen miles South of St. Augustine.
- -	-	1792	P. Marrot -	River. St. John's.
Estralgo -	-	- -	- -	Ocklewaha, on St John's River.
Coppinger	-	- -	- -	This land was first situated on the River St. Mary's; and afterwards, by the Governor's permission, transferred to the 12 mile Swamp.
- -	-	- -	G. J. F. Clarke	McGirt's Creek, St. John's River.
- -	-	- 1821	A. Burgevin -	River St. John's.
White -	1790	- -	- -	Amelia Island.
- -	-	- -	- -	British grant, situated on Nassau River
White -	1790	- -	- -	Musquitoe.
- -	-	Jan. 25, 1818	R. McHardy -	Musquitoe.
Coppinger	-	- -	- -	Turnbull's Swamp.
Same -	1790	- -	- -	An Island on St. John's River.
White -	-	- -	- -	Musquitoe.
White -	1790	- -	- -	Musquitoe.
White -	1790	- -	- -	Musquitoe.
White -	1790	- -	- -	South of the town of Mantanzas.
White -	1790	- -	- -	Mantanzas.

* In two tracts of 250 and 150 acres.

† This claim was rejected by former Board.

‡ This claim is in two surveys.

REPORT No. 2—Continued.

Numbers.	NAMES OF PRESENT CLAIMANTS.	NAMES OF ORIGINAL CLAIMANTS.	Date of Patent or Royal Title.	Date of Concession, or order of Survey.	Quantity of Land. Acres. hdths.
86	Buyck & Dupont -	Buyck & Dupont -	- -	1794	Undefined
87	James McGirt - -	James McGirt -	- -	1796	-
*88	Same - -	Same -	- -	1792	500.00
*89	Same - -	Same -	- -	1793	300.00
*90	Same - -	Same -	- -	1798	80.00
91	Same - -	Same -	- -	1799	500.00
92	Same - -	Same -	- -		
93	Same - -	Same -	- -	- -	600.00
94	D. McGirt, the son -	D. McGirt, the son	- -	1797	200.00
95	Sarah Tate - -	Edward Tate -	- -	1803	450 00
96	John Gaudry - -	John Gaudry -	- -	Oct'r 6, 1807	3,000.00
97	P. Mitchell, and others	John McClure -	-	-	550.00
98	Hibberson & Yonge -	Hibberson & Yonge	- -	Jan. 25, 1810	45.00
99	Robert Hutchinson -	R. Hutchinson -	- -	1816	150.00
100	Samuel King - -	Samuel King -	- -	1804	300.00
101	Widow and heirs of Antonio Martinez -	Anto. Martinez -	- -	June 3, 1806	70.00
102	Robert Pritchard's heirs	R. Pritchard -	- -	1800	700.00
103	Gachalan Vass - -	G. Vass - -	- -	1793	250.00
104	James Tool - -	James Tool -	- -	1803	945.00
105	Francis Triay - -	Francis Triay -	- -	1802	-
106	William Traverse -	John McQueen -	- -	1799	100 00
107	Isaac Tucker - -	Isaac Tucker -	- -	1804	200.00
108	Gabriel Triay - -	Gabriel Triay -	- -	Jan. 2, 1818	-
109	Farquhar Bethune -	Farquhar Bethune	- -	Aug. 25, 1815	172.00
110	Thomas Backhouse -	Thomas Backhouse	June 20, 1818	-	500.00
111	Wm. H. G. Saunders	John Saunders -	- -	1791	1,200.00
112	W. Travers, agent, &c.	—— Yellowly -	1777	- -	500.00
†113	William Dry - -	Alexander Gray -	1771	-	1,000.00
†114	Same -	Lots in the City of St. Augustine			
†115	Same -				
†116	Andrew Atkinson -	A. Atkinson -	- -	1792	100.00
117	Heirs of Anto. Andrew	Antonio Andrew -	- -	1796	500.00
118	John Jones - -	John Jones -	- -	Feb'ry, 1801	500.00
119	Ezekiel Tucker -	E. Tucker -	- -	Mar. 18, 1817	150.00
120	Stephen Eubank -	Stephen Eubank -	- -	Feb. 4, 1806	255.00
121	P. Dupon - -	P. Dupon -	- -	Oct. 8, 1817	3,000.00
122	M. Villalonga - -	M Villalonga -	- -	Oct. 24, 1801	10.00
123	Same - -	Same -	- -	Nov. 10, 1790	6.00
124	Pablo F. Fontane -	Pablo F. Fontane -	- -	May 15, 1815	3,000.00
125	Jacob Worldly -	Jacob Worldly -	- -	Nov. 1806	Undefined
126	Ezekiel Tucker -	E Tucker -	-	1805	100.00
127	P. Peso de Burgo -	P. P. de Burgo -	-	April, 1815	400.00
128	Hannah Smith - -	Hannah Smith -	- -	1817	400.00
129	Charles Gobert -	Charles Gobert -	-	Nov. 1804	2,000.00
130	Joseph M. Hernandez	J. M. Hernandez -	April 8, 1818	- -	Undefined
131	Sebastian Garcia -	S. Garcia -	-	Nov. 9, 1792	15.00
132	Same - -	Same -	-	1802	6.00

The three claims marked thus, (*) have been confirmed.—See Report and Abstract, A.

The four do marked thus, (†) are British grants

REPORT No. 2—Continued.

By whom conceded.	Authority or Royal Order under which the concession was granted.	Date of Survey.	By whom Surveyed.	WHERE SITUATED.
Quesada -	-	- -	- -	A small Island between the two bars of the River Mantanzas
Same -				
Same -	1790	- -	- -	A part on Suwannee Creek, and a part on Nassau River.
Same -	1790	- -	- -	St. Mary's River.
Same -	1790	- -	- -	St. Mary's River.
White -	1790	- -	- -	St. Mary's River.
- -	-	1792	P. Marrot -	Andrew's Point, on St. John's River.
White -	1790	- -	- -	St. Mary's River.
White -	1790	- -	- -	On Tomoco.
Coppinger	1790	- -	- -	Spring Garden.
- -	-	- -	- -	Ocklewaha.
White -	1790	- -	- -	Amelia Island.
Coppinger	1790	-	- -	Little St. Mary's Swamp.
White -	1790	- -	- -	River Nassau.
White -	1790	- -	- -	Moultree Creek.
White -	1790	- -	- -	Goodsby's Lake.
- -	-	- -	P. Marrot -	Pablo Creek.
White -	1790	- -	- -	Graham's Swamp.
White -	1790	- -	- -	North River.
White -	1790	- -	- -	Pottsburgh Creek.
White -	1790	- -	- -	St. John's River.
Coppinger	1816	- -	- -	Key Bacas.
Estrada -	1790	- -	- -	Spell's Swamp, River Nassau.
Coppinger	1815	- -	- -	Indian River.
Quesada -	1790	- -	- -	St. John's River.
Tonyn -	-	- -	- -	Derbin Swamp.
Grant -	-	- -	- -	East fork Diego River.
Quesada -	-	- -	- -	St. Vincent Ferrier.
Quesada -	-	- -	- -	New Smyrna.
White -	1790	- -	- -	St. John's River.
Coppinger	1790	- -	- -	Nassau River, Tucker's Creek.
White -	1790	- -	- -	Bounded by the lands of E. Tucker.
Coppinger	1790	- -	- -	Spring Garden.
White -	1790	- -	- -	Without the gates of St. Augustine.
- -	-	- -	- -	Same place.
Kindelan -	1815	- -	- -	Vackasa Creek.
White -	1790	- -	- -	Trout Creek.
White -	1790	- -	-	Nassau.
Kindelan -	1815	- -	- -	St. John's River.
Coppinger	1790	- -	- -	Deep Creek.
White -	1790	- -	- -	Dunn's Island, St. John's River.
Coppinger	1790	- -	- -	A marsh in front of his farm.
Quesada -	1790	- -	- -	Outside of the gates of St. Augustine.
White -	1790	- -	- -	Same place.

C. DOWNING.
W. H. ALLEN.

REPORT, NO. 3.

No. 1.

JAMES DAILEY, *Claimant—23,000 acres of land, on Dunn's Lake.*

An application for six miles square on Dunn's Lake, in absolute property, to establish a saw mill. The decree is dated on the 10th November, 1817, and makes the grant *in absolute property.*

We have already said, that there is no permission to erect a mill over which a deep suspicion does not rest, which passes the title to the soil, and does not prescribe that the grant is void, unless the mill is erected. This grant conveys more land than any other of the kind. It is for six miles square; and G. Clarke certifies that he surveyed to the claimant, in December, 1817, 23,000 acres of land. We do not believe this grant is valid. It is Aguillar's certificate of title, and nothing more. It is rejected.

No. 2.

JOSPPH DALESPINE, *Claimant—43,000 acres of land.*

No. 3.

Same, for 10,244 acres of land.

The first is for services, for various sums of money which he claims of the Royal Finance, for supplies, provisions, &c. and thirdly, for the losses which he has sustained during the years of 1813 and 14, for his loyalty, &c. This appears by the memorial of the claimant to the Governor, April 6th, 1817; in which he also states that, for all these, he had received no recompense. He thererore prays for 50,000 acres, in fee simple, on the West side of Indian river, or river Ys, opposite Marratt's Island. On the 9th of the same month, Coppinger decreed that 43,000 acres should be granted.

This is Thomas Aguilar's certificate. We cannot recognize this grant as valid. Coppinger was liberal enough, bnt Aguilar would make him boundlessly extravagant. It is rejected.

There is on the back of the Spanish certificate of title, an acknowledgment from Dalespine, that he holds one half of the land claimed, in trust for Michael Tagarges, of Charleston, and a covenant to convey it to any one whom the said Tagarges may designate.

No. 3. Pablo Fontane, of whom Dalespine is a purchaser, produces the certificate of T. Aguilar, to this effect: that, in 1817, he, Fontane, presented his memorial to the Governor, stating, that, as others had obtained lands for services, he had formerly procured a grant of four miles square, on Trout Creek, which, when examined, was found to be private property; wherefore, he wishes to locate the grant on Indian river. The Governor assented to the proposal. It does not appear that the original of Aguilar's certificate, or the papers of the first grant on Trout Creek, said to be returned, are found in the proper office. But, in 1820, there is another petition and memorial of Fontane, for a survey. The decree is favorable, and we believe the signature is the Governor's own hand writing. It is, furthermore, certified by Entralgo, and we can have no doubt that the grant was made. Andrew Burgevin, by direction, surveyed it. This grant will depend for its decision solely on the power of the Governor, on which point, we have already expressed our opinion. We should have remarked, that Fontane styled himself a merchant in this case, as does Dalespine himself in the preceeding.

No. 4.

EUSEBIO MARIA GOMEZ, *Claimant—12,000 acres of land.*

Thomas de Aguillar, Secretary of Government, certifies that, on the 15th day of July, 1815, Eusebio Maria Gomez presented a memorial, praying for 12,000 acres of land, for services and head rights, situated on the rivers Jupiter and Santa Lucias, including the old English settlements on said rivers. To which Governor Estrada made the following decree, on the 16th of the above month and year: "Let there be granted to the interested, on the terms which he indicates, the lands which he solicits, in the place pointed out, without injury to a third person, as the services which he states, are well known to this Government; and that this gift may be made known, let there be issued to him, from the Secretary's office, the corresponding certificate." We have always required the party to shew some cause, however slight, for the loss of the original of Aguillar's certificate. This is not attempted; and, independent of all other grounds of objection, on this alone, we would reject the claim.

No. 5.

DANIEL O'HARA, *Claimant—15,000 acres of land.*

Thomas de Aguillar, Secretary of Government, certifies that Daniel O' Hara presented a memorial, dated September 3, 1803, soliciting 15,000 acres of land, (vacant) situated at a place called Nassau, between the rivers St. John's and St. Mary's, when the survey takes place. Gov. White passes the memorial to the Commandant of Engineers for his report; agreeably to which, Governor White made the following decree, dated the 5th of the same month and year: "Let there be granted to this interested, the land which he solicits, without injury to a third person; and, until, according to the number of workers he may have for its cultivation, there shall be measured what he is entitled to; it being well understood that he cannot claim damages for injuries, in case that, from fear of an invasion, or other motives, of the Royal service, he be ordered to retire into the interior of the province; and that he must take possession of the said land in the space of six months from the date."

This, if genuine, of which we are not satisfied, is a mere grant for head rights, and is a bare declaration that, when he proved the number of his family, he should have surveyed to him as many acres, as, by the regulations, he was entitled to. It does not appear that he proceeded to perfect his title, or to ascertain the number of acres, or to to cultivate and possess it. Rejected.

No. 6.

PHILIP R. YOUNG, *Claimant—25,000 acres of land.*

This is a plain royal title, made by Governor Coppinger in 1816, for services.

The land in the grant, is located at Spring Garden, and subdivided as follows: 12,000 in the neighborhood of a lake named Second, and known as Valdey's; and the remaining 13,000 at a larger lake higher up, known as Long lake; all on the West side of the river St. John. If the Governor had power to make so large a grant, this is good; but, as our opinion is adverse, we cannot recommend it.

No. 7.

GEORGE FLEMING'S *heirs, Claimants—20,000 acres of land.*

This land lies on Indian river, at the mouth of St. Sebastian's river. There is a royal title in 1816, for services. If the Governor had power to make so large a grant, this is a good one.

No. 8.

ANTONIO ACOSTA, *Claimant—8,000 acres of land.*

This is another of Aguilar's certificates, without an original. In May, 1816, "as he has been a constant resident at Fernandina; being continually employed in mercantile pursuits; has served whenever the Governor thought proper; has been ready with his person, funds, and influence, in the defence, &c. of this town, (Fernandina); has never received any salary, &c. for his expenses, supplies, and losses; and has refrained from troubling the Government with his importunities," he prays for 8,000 acres of land.

But as he is ignorant of the lands that are vacant, and wishes to avoid disputes, he prays the Governor "will be pleased approve the surveys, whenever the Surveyor General shall have done so, on vacant lands."

The grant is made with special directions to the Surveyor General, to have them surveyed.

If this grant was evidently genuine, we should deem it incomplete. It is a promise to recognise a survey when made, and a power given to make it. There is no evidence that the survey was made—there is no pretence, that it was recognised when made, and the grant consummated by such recognition. It is true, that, in the memorial to this Board, he says, "the land was surveyed in the usual manner pursued by Mr. Clark: 1,500 acres in Jobing Hammock; 1,500 acres on the north of Dun's creek; and 1,000 acres at Bowley's old field, with a tender of those surveys when required." The surveys are not produced, and if there was no objection to the grant, on the proof of its genuineness, we should require some evidence, that the surveys were shewn to the Governor, and approved and ratified. It is rejected.

No. 9.

FRANCES J. AVICE, *Claimant*—500 *acres of land.*

This is a part of grant of 30,000 acres made to ——— Arredondo, and confirmed by Board of Land Commissioners. We have no wish or power to sever it from the larger grant. The one will decide the fate of both.

No. 10.

FRANCISCA AGUILAR, *Claimant*—30,000 *acres of land.*

It appears that the petitioner possessed a certificate of Thomas Aguilar, and presented it to the Governor of Cuba in 1823, with a request that a certified copy of Aguilar's certificate should be made by the Notary of Cuba, and the original, *to wit:* Aguilar's certificate, returned to her. This is done with all the imposing pomp of the seal notarial, &c.; but it amounts simply to this: That, in 1815, Aguilar certifies that Governor Quesada, in 1794, on the 24th of February, granted to the petitioner in absolute property, 30,000 acres of land, at a place called Haw creek, situated to the south of the river St. John, about twelve miles distant from.

Let us look at the memorial on which the grant is made. In 1794, Don Juan Rodriguez states, "that, having a sufficient number of slaves to dedicate himself to agriculture, and the raising of horned cattle, and also to aid in the maintenance of his large family," he hopes that his Excellency, following the spirit of royal orders, which protects the Spanish inhabitants, who have sacrificed themselves in the service of the said province, during the *turbulent times* which have taken place in it; your memorialist having been one of *its defenders;* for which reason, he prays," &c.

Now, every remark made by us, in the case of the two Arredondos, will apply with double force to the case before us; with this essential difference against this claim, that, in 1794, when this grant bears date, we do not believe that any disturbance whatever had taken place in this province. In 1796, there was a small rising on the St. John's River; and the Arredondos may claim that services were rendered at that period. But, here is a bold appeal in 1794, to the Governor, to reward services performed "during the "turbulent periods which have taken place in it;" and there was no turbulence until 1796; "following the spirit, (we use the words of the memorial) of the royal orders, which protects the Spanish inhabitants, who have sacrificed themselves in the service of the province;" such, in 1794, is an appeal to the provisions of a law passed in 1815. We are unwilling, by any opinion of ours, liable as we may be to error, to debar any individual from a redress in the Courts of his country. We will not, therefore, pronounce this grant a fraud or forgery; but we unhesitatingly reject it.

No. 11.

GEORGE ATKINSON, *Claimant*—15,000 *acres of land.*

George Atkinson petitions the Government, on the 8th October, 1816, for 15,000 acres of land in Cedar Swamp, and on the West side of a lake called Upper Little Lake, for his services during the years 1812, 1813, 1814, and 1815; to which, Governor Coppinger made the following decree, on the 20th of the above month and year: "Taking into consideration the merits, as set forth by Don George Atkinson, and the benign will of his Majesty, requiring that his meritorious subjects be rewarded, I grant him possession, and, without injury to a third person, of the lands which he solicits in his memorial; and, agreeably to which, the Surveyor General will survey the same in the place he points out, or in others that may be vacant, and being in places equally advantageous.

"COPPINGER."

No. 12.

GEORGE ATKINSON, *Claimant—4,000 acres of land.*

This grant bears date February, 1810. It is first certified by Thomas de Aguilar, and, afterwards, by Juan de Entralgo, as on file among the papers under his charge, as Escrivano. Mr. Fatio, the Clerk of this Board, certifies that the original of the paper produced itself, evidently, a copy is on file, in the Office of the Public Archives.

Meranda, from whom Atkinson purchased, petitioned for this land, for his services, as a place on which to work his negroes. It seems strange that Governor White, whose rigorous refusal to give large portions of land is so remarkable, should break down a settled principle of action, more than once, in favor of this individual; Meranda was, as he declares in some of his memorials to the Governor, the second Pilot of the Bar. If we credit the document here produced and filed, to this second Pilot, Governor White, after having already granted 368,000 acres for his extraordinary services, gives, in addition, the 4,000 acres claimed as above. In addition to all this, the grant is made for services in 1811; and the law authorizing such grants, was passed in 1815. On this subject, we beg leave to refer to our remarks in the case of Arredondo, of this Abstract, No. 15. We cannot recommend it.

No. 13.

F. M. ARREDONDO & SON, *Claimants—38,000 acres of land.*

A grant by concession, of 38,000 acres of land, "situated on both banks of a creek which empties into the Suwannee River, called Alligator Creek, commencing seven miles West of the Indian village called Alligator Town, about forty miles from Paynes Town, and eighty miles from Buenavista, known under the denomination of Alachua.

The petitioner declares his services, and the increased number of his hands, as an inducement for the grant; and it is made by Governor Coppinger, "in absolute proprietorship." On the 24th March, 1817, at a subsequent period, Andrew Bergevin was authorized to survey the land, but it does not appear to have been done. We have no doubt but this grant is genuine; and the sole question to be decided is, as to the power of the Governor. We have already given our views on this point. If we are right, the claim will be rejected, unless Arredondo had the requisite number of workers to entitle him to so large a grant. It will be submitted to the courts of the country, for a final decision.

No. 14.

F. M. Arredondo, *Claimant—50,000 acres of land.*

This grant is similar in all its parts to the preceding; it is dated in 1810. It is certified by Aguilar, in the first instance, by Philip Alvaris afterwards, whose character for good faith and credit, judicially and extrajudicially," is avouched by the same witnesses notarial, as in the other following this; it comes from the same offices; it is signed by the same Governor; it is granted for services, under the order of 1790, in the same form and manner as the preceding; it is then liable to the same objections, and must share the same fate. We cannot recommend it.

No. 15.

J. M. Arredondo, *Claimant—40,000 acres of land.*

The title paper in this case, is an unqualified and unconditional Royal title, purporting to have been made by Governor White, on the 12th day of January, 1811. The preamble declares that, Whereas Don Joseph de la Mazo Arredondo, a *subject* of his Catholic Majesty, resident and merchant of this city, &c., has represented, &c., praying for a concession of 40,000 acres, in absolute property, at a place called Oquilabaga, &c. In consequence of the merits, and the well *known services* of the petitioner, rendered by his person and property, during the unfortunate period under which this part of his dominions labored; and, at the same time, according to what is set forth in the Royal order of 1790, relative to the granting of lands free of expense to *new settlers:* wherefore, and being known to me, the merits and laudable services of the memorialist, I have thought proper to grant, &c. the 40,000 acres solicited, &c. The residue of this grant is in the usual form. The genuineness of this grant is evidenced, by the certificate of Thomas de Aguilar, and subsequently, on the 18th March, 1819, by the certificate of Filipe Alvarez, that this is in conformity with the original on file in the Notary Public's office at Havana, and of Don Joseph Leal, that he, Alvarez, is another notary. If this grant, either by copy, or original, was ever on file in the archives in this city, it has not been made known to the Board, nor is there any attempt made to account for the strange fact, that the original of a grant to land in Florida should be on file in the Havana, and not in the city of St. Augustine.

There are many objections to this grant, besides the want of power in the Governor to depart from the line of his instructions, as laid down by the Royal orders under which he acted:

1st, The bare certificate of Aguilar is not sufficient to justify us in recommending for confirmation.

2d, It is suspicious that this grant and this certificate should be found in Cuba, without a trace of it remaining here. It was made, if made at all, by White, the Governor here; Aguilar was the Secretary here; here was the land, and here all similar records were deposited. We should require that some satisfactory reason should be given, for the departure, in this case, from a rule almost universal. Great care was taken by the American Commissioners, at the change of the flags, that the titles to property should not be removed to Havana; and it is believed, that care, accompanied by some violence, was effectual.

3d, Governor White was more rigorously exact in granting lands, than any who preceded or came after him. His regulations are exact and precise, and his official declaration uniform and peremptory on this subject; and we doubt whether there is one single exception to Governor White's adhesion to the rules which he had prescribed for himself, *under the provisions* of the law, unaccompanied by positive suspicion of unfairness.

4th, The grant is made under the order of 1790, "relative to strangers;" Arredondo was a "resident and subject." The order of 1790, requires that lands should be granted in proportion to the workers: here nothing is said of workers, but it is granted for services. Now, whatever may have been the practice of his successors, we doubt that Governor White ever granted lands for a particular reason, and cited the law in the body of the grant, as his authority, directly adverse to the authority claimed.

5th, This grant was made "for the merits and well known services of the petitioner," in 1811; and the law giving authority to reward services, by grants of land, was passed in 1815; and the war which gave occasion to the law, commenced in 1812.

We are not disposed to pronounce on the authenticity of this grant, so as to bar the claimant from his remedy in a court of law, but we cannot recommend it for confirmation.

No. 16.

F. M. Arredondo, *Claimant—250,000 acres of land.*

This is one of Aguilar's certificates, dated on the 2d April, 1809. It states, "That to the memorial of the claimant of the same date, soliciting, in virtue of their merits and services, which rendered in favor of his Majesty, in the city, with his person and his property, the concession, in absolute property, of ten miles to each cardinal point of the compass, of vacant lands, at a place called *Calaso Gachey* in the Spiritu Santo, its boundary running from the river of the same name to the river Manaty, in consequence of this solicitude, the following decree was this day made known thereon." "Being, as they are, evident to this Government, the merits and recommendable services. rendered by the interested, in this representatation, I have thought proper to grant him, as in the name of his Majesty, I do grant him, in absolute property, the said ten miles of land, in a square, for himself, his heirs, and successors." "Without the necessity of any other title, separating the royal domain from the right and dominion which it had to said lands, ceding and transferring them to the said Arrendondo, his heirs, and successors, that, as their own, they may use and enjoy them without any incumbrance whatever, with all its entrances, outlets, uses, and customs, and every thing else that belongs to it by right; and for his security and confirmation in any event, the Secretary of Government shall despatch to him the corresponding certificate.

WHITE.

And, in compliance with what is ordered in the preceding superior decree, I give the present in St. Augustine, Florida, the 2d day of April, 1809. THOMAS DE AGUILAR."

There is a copy of the memorial and decree forwarded from the City of Havana, with another certificate of Aguilar, dated on the 5th January, 1824, that the original remained in the hands of the claimant. The evidence in support of the claim is this—The deposition of the same Aguilar, taken by interrogatories, directed to Havana, and the affidavit of William Reynolds, late keeper of the public archives of this city. Aguilar recollects perfectly of making the grant, and swears to the power of Governor White to do so. He gives his opinion that a copy of the grant may be found, in the office of Vedal, of that city, and swears that the copy, heretofore spoken of, is a correct one; that the grant was not only legal, but from the services of Arredondo to the Government, highly merited. All of which facts and circumstances he is fully acquainted with, having been for many years Secretary to the Government. When cross examined, he says, it was not a general custom to have grants for lands in Florida recorded in Havana, and that the copy of this grant was there recorded lest it should be lost or mislaid." "A course not necessary, but optional with the parties, grants being universally recorded in Florida, where the lands lay." He then deposes, that the copy of which we have spoken is a correct one.

William Reynolds, in his affidavit, before a Justice of the Peace, deposes, that he had seen in the office of Mr. Law, late alcalde, a paper purporting to be a grant to F. D. Arredondo, Jr. by Governor White, for a large tract of land in East Florida, which said document has not been in the possession of the affiant, as keeper of the public archives. One-fourth part of this land has been sold by Claimant to Moses E. Levy, by deed bearing date 4th January, 1822.

From the abstract of the documents and testimony rendered as above, the opinion of this Board must be against this claim. It is a certificate of Tho. Aguilar, with a certified copy of that certificate from Havana, where the grant, properly, never should have been recorded. It is a grant made for services in 1809, six years before the royal order of 1815, the only authority that we know of, given to the Governors of East Florida, to reward the services of subjects, by the donation of lands. It is said to be made by Gov. White, who was more rigorously exact in conforming to the laws and ordinances, and more parsimonious in his grants, than any Governor who preceded or came after him. It is made in absolute property, which was never done and could never be done, until the royal order of 1815—and to a man, who, by the evidence before the Board, was twenty-one years of age at the date of the grant, and a minor by the Spanish Laws. We will not by our sentence preclude the party from going before the Courts, but we cannot recommend it for confirmation.

No. 17.

Peter Merando, *Claimant—368,640 acres of land.*

As this is a large grant, and one which has been much spoken of, we shall give at length the petition of the party, and the decree of the Governor.

Senor Governor: Don Pedro Merando, second pilot of the launch of the bar of this port, with the most profound respect, states to your Excellency, That he has had the honor to serve his most Catholic Majesty (whom God preserve) from the year 1788, when he was employed as a rower in said launch; in which capacity he continued, until, by his distinguished merits and skill, he was appointed to his present employment. Farthermore, your Excellency well knows the truth of his good management, fidelity, and love of the service of his Majesty, proved in divers expeditions, which, by order of this Government, the deponent made in the year 1795, in the rivers of this province, when it was ravaged by the rebels; and as for such remarkable services, and others latterly performed, to the satisfaction of your Excellency: Wherefore, he prays your Excellency to be pleased, in recompense of what he has set forth, and in consideration of his impoverished situation, to grant him an absolute property, eight leagues square, in the royal lands which are on the waters of the bays of Hillsborough and Tampor, in this province, by virtue of the royal orders for the granting of lands gratis, to the Spanish subjects, a favor which he hopes to obtain from the justice of your Excellency. St. Augustine, Florida, the 19th of November, 1810—Pedro Merando.—St. Augustine, Florida, 26th November, 1810. The merits and services which this party sets forth, being well known and established, let there be granted to him on the terms which he solicits, the quantity, of land at the points indicated, without injury to a third person, and to authenticate this grant, at all times, let a certified copy of this memorial be issued from the Secretary's office for his security.—WHITE."

The witnesses examined in this case before the former Board of Commssioners, are Gabriel W. Perpall, F. Bethune, James Hall, Antonio Alverez, and B. Segue. The only point upon which their examination goes, is the authenticity of the original and the signature of Governor White. Perpall says that "it looks like the signature of White, but he cannot swear to it." "That, from the finishing of the flourish attached to the name, he cannot believe or disbelieve it to be genuine, as the difference might arise from the position in which the writer's hand was placed, or from some other cause."

Carrado has never seen the Governor write, and knows nothing about it.

Bethune does "not think the writing as perfect as Governor White's signature usually was, the Governor being remarkable for great precision therein; but it may, nevertheless, be his, as it may have been written when he was unwell." When cross-examined, he says, "the Governor died in 1811, and had been indisposed several months before his death, but was not confined to his bed." That he had seen the Governor sign different decrees, some of which were for land, and some for passports, but *neither*, within a few months before his death." When asked whether he had seen Governor White write on any other occasion than those mentioned above, so as to enable him to acquire a knowledge of the Governor's hand writing, he answered in the negative. He says, furthermore, "That the Governor, a few years before his death, drank a little hard in the afternoon, though he did not usually transact business at that time." The witness, in 1810, lived on the river St. John's, and came occasionally to town.

James Hall was acquainted with the Governor from 1798 until 1810, and "has often seen him write." When the original was presented to him, he says, "The signature of White looks something like the Governor's, but witness had never seen any of his writing done so incorrectly as this." That his opinion is formed "from the latter part of the name, *White*, which appears to have been written lower down than was usual with the Governor." "That this is the only material difference perceived by the witness, though the whole does not appear so correct as he, White, usually wrote."

The above witnesses seem to have been sworn on the part of the United States, and those that follow on the part of the claimant. Antonio Alverez deposes, "That he is acquainted with the hand writing of Governor White. That he has been a clerk in his office, in which situation he has often seen him write. That he entered said office in the year 1807, and continued there, with two slight intermissions, until the change of flags in 1821," when the original concessions, brought before the Board, from the office of the public archives, by the keeper thereof, was exhibited to the witness, and he was asked whether he believed the signature "*White,*" to be genuine; he answered simply in the affirmative. When cross-examined he deposes, "That his opinion of the genuineness of the signature is formed both from the signature itself and the flourish immediately under it." "He has no particular recollection of the Ts or the Es, in Governor White's name, or the manner in which the first was crossed, or the second joined to it, but from the general appearance of the signature, believes it to be genuine." He does not believe the E is made totally different from the manner in which Governor White usually made it, but it seems closer to the T than Governor White placed it usually; that the Governor signed his name with great uniformity, and he considers this signature regular and uniform."

The witness knows nothing of the making of this grant He says that concessions for lands were deposited in the Government Secretary's office. When asked if it was within his knowledge, that, since the time at which this concession was made, it had always been in the said office, he adverted to the date of the concession, and answered in the affirmative. He furthermore deposes, that vacant lands, situated at a distance from St. Augustine, were not considered of much value or importance about the year 1810: and, to the question of the District Attorney, he answers, "That Governor White was always cautious and sparing in granting to individuals any part of the public lands." B. Segue "is well acquainted with the hand-writing of Governor White, having seen him write many times." Witness lived in the Government Notary's office, from whence it was his duty, almost every day, to carry papers to the Governor for his signature. In this office he continued, with a few intermissions, from the year 1800 to the year 1812 or 1813. When the grant now under adjudication was presented to him, and he was asked whether he believed the signature to be genuine, he answers, "that he has no doubt of it." He says further, "that he became acquainted with the existence of this grant a few days after it was made, as he (the witness) drew the memorial at the request of Mr. Merando: and that the lands, situated at such a distance from St. Augustine as those granted by this concession, were then considered of very little value.

On a question of the District Attorney, whether the Governors of this then Province were not regulated in the distribution of lands to individuals, more by the principles and rules they had adopted and established for the granting of lands than the value of lands granted? the witness answers, "That the Governors were regulated, in the granting of lands, by the merits of the individual, the number of his family, or the value of the lands asked for, according to his own discretion." We have thus given, at full length, the documentary evidence upon which this claim is based, and an abstract of the evidence taken before the Board of Commissioners, nearly as long as the depositions themselves, adopting, for the most part, the language of the witnesses; not that we have deemed this testimony at all important to the decision of the case, if our decision was final, but it may be satisfactory to the numerous claimants under the pretended grantee. It seems to us strange that the name of White should be attached to a grant like this, whose uniform practice and unvarying declarations have shewn, in the language of the witness Alverez, "that he was always cautious and sparing in granting to individuals any part of the public lands." There are many letters of Governor White to the Superintendent at Cuba. There are many of his decrees and regulations, in all of which he has invariably declared, that he would conform to the laws in granting of lands. Nay, more, he has, by his own act, made those laws more rigorous than they were, and circumscribed within narrow limits his own authority. He has said in his letter to the Governor General of Cuba, that the regulations of Quesada were too liberal, in granting one hundred acres to the heads of families, and one half of that quantity to its members; and by his (Governor White's) own decree, he has reduced the relative quantity to 50 and 25 acres.

If we examine the laws of Spain, we shall see by the laws of the Indies, published in the recent copy of the land laws, page ——, and in the Royal order of 1754, so much spoken of, published in the same book, for the first time, page ——: we shall find by those laws, that no authority is given for a grant like this. The only subsequent decree upon the subject of land, which we have been enabled to discover, is the Royal order of 1790, made specially for this Province. That order applies exclusively to foreigners; and it was a matter of courtesy on the part of the Governors, to extend its provisions to the native subjects of Spain. It has been contended that, by the provisions of that order, there is no fixed quantity of acres named, to which the party should be entitled; or, in other words, the power of the Governor, upon that subject, is left without limit. Without adverting to the many declarations of his Catholic Majesty, made in his Royal orders, of dates both previous and subsequent, that lands should be granted in proportion to the workers of a family, or, in other words, that no man should have granted to him more lands than he could cultivate; and, furthermore, that lands should only be given for the sake of cultivation and improvement, and not for the sake of speculation: we might admit, for the sake of argument, that the quantity to be granted was left only to the Governor's discretion. That discretion has been exercised by Governor Quesada, in the first place, and afterwards by Governor White. This last Governor, in his letter to the Marquis De Someruelos, the Captain General of Cuba, dated 15th October, 1803, uses these words: "My predecessor has assigned one hundred acres of land to the fathers of families, and fifty to each child or slave, whether full grown or small, a quantity really excessive, and could only have taken place at that time in which there were few strangers who came in solicitude of lands; but at present there are many who come, and, consequently, there would result the greatest injury in the improvement of the Province, unless said number of acres be diminished, on account of its being more than one individual can cultivate in a year, even divided into three parts, for the purpose of giving rest to the lands. Which circumstance I have had also present for the deduction which has been made."

After this, it is impossible for us to believe that Governor White, either *before or after dinner*, ever made a grant of 368,640 acres of land to any individual whatever. The grantee cannot claim the land under the laws of the Indies, or the royal orders of 1754 or 1790, and we know of no authority vested in the Spanish Governor, before the year 1815, to make a grant to any individual for services, however much more than Governor W. that governor may have been disposed to be liberal.

If we look at the grant itself, and take the claim and merits of Merando, as set forth by himself, to be true, how contemptible and ridiculous do they seem, when viewed as a basis for a grant like this. P. Merando, second pilot of the launch of the bar of this port, promoted by his distinguished merits and skill, from a common rower on board of said launch, claims a principality as his reward. In addition to high services as pilot and rower, he represents that he has made some magnificent expeditions in the rivers of this province, and then, for his services and his poverty, modestly begs for eight leagues square, by virtue of the royal orders for the granting of lands gratis to Spanish subjects.

We will not pronounce this grant a forgery, and thus debar the party of the rights which he may have acquired by the law of 23d May, 1828. We are prevented from this by the deposition of Segue and Alvarez; but we think it our duty to say, that we view any grant purporting to be made by Governor White to a larger amount than is prescribed by the Royal orders. and by his own regulation, as extremely suspicious. We consider him the most correct Governor who has ever presided in East Florida, the most strictly observant of the laws, and the most parsimonious of the public lands; and we do firmly believe, that, if his example had been followed by his successors, *and if his name had never been signed after his death*, there would now be no confusion in the land titles of East Florida. We furthermore believe, that, previous to the year 1803, Governor White never made a grant of land more extensive than that prescribed by the regulations of Quesada; nor, subsequently to that period, more extensive than was permitted by his own. We do not believe that he has ever yet made a grant for services, nor for any thing other than head rights; that he has never made a grant, *when living*, of 20,000 acres to one individual, whatever he may have done since dead: and that he has never made a grant within the Indian boundaries, within which limits this land then lay. It is true that the original of this document, or claim, has been found in the office of the Public Archives, but it is a matter of history, that the papers now deposited there were, for a long time after the change of government, most loosely kept and guarded: and it was a matter of equal facility to take a paper out, or smuggle it in. From the best evidence we have been enabled to acquire upon this subject, it appears to the Board that there were two offices at this place under the Spanish Government: The Escribano office, which was regularly kept in books, stitched together in consecutive pages, with all the records closely following each other, so as to make it extremely difficult to interpolate a grant. For the records of this office we have high respect; it seems to have been a place where all grants were recorded when fully matured. The other, the office of the Governor's Secretary, was of a different character; here, all the papers were in loose and detached sheets, easy to have been taken away, or to have had a forged document thrust among them, without the power of detection. This is the office in which all the memorials for lands, with the inchoate decree of the Governor, were first thrown; and it does appear to the Board, that these first decrees do, in no case, amount to a grant, but barely give to the applicant the right to become a settler upon the performance of all the conditions imposed by the law. We will give an exemplification of our ideas: A. B. upon coming into the province, if he is a new settler, writes his memorial to the Governor, and applies for 50,000 acres of land; the Governor says, "let it be granted, until, according to the number of his family, the portion to which he is entitled is allotted to him." This paper is thrown into the Governor's Secretary's Office, and, as we conceive, is itself no record, and conveys no title. It is a bare permission to the applicant to settle in the country, and to receive his lands if he shall take the oath of allegiance; 50,000 acres if he has workers enough to justify the grant, and 500 if, by the number of his family, he is entitled to no more. It will not be pretended that the party could claim the lands thus granted, if he never afterwards took the oath of allegiance, nor can it be pretended that, by the mere grant, as above supposed, the 50,000 acres are conveyed, until some subsequent step is taken by the party to consummate his title. In addition to the oath of allegiance, he was required to swear to the number of his workers; and, when this was done, *according to the number* of his workers *was the quantity granted*, and subsequently surveyed by the public surveyor. Then it was that the documents were all transferred to the office of the Escribano, fairly written out in a book of records, and entitled to the fullest confidence; but the loose papers in the Governor's Secretary's office, the first memorial and decree, such as we have just described it, do not seem to have conveyed any title, to have been considered any record, or worthy of any preservation. It was over this last office that Thomas de Aguilar presided; it is from this office that so many monstrous grants have emanated; it is from this office that the originals of Thomas de Aguilar's certificates of grants are lost; and it is in this office that the original of the grant before us is to be found. It may be, as well from the loose manner in which these documents in the Governor's Secretary's office were kept, as from the little faith to be attached to Aguilar's certificates, that so many of the originals of those certificates are lost; and, if the view which we have taken of this matter be correct, Aguilar may have been a meritorious officer, his certificates perfectly genuine, and the grants which are pretended to be conveyed by them of no validity. It is possible that, after making the application for the lands, as certified by Aguilar, the party, unable or unwilling to comply with the conditions, had abandoned his intention of becoming a Spanish subject, and a Spanish grantee, and yet, having scrupulously preserved the certificate of Aguilar, given at the time when the original, known to be of no value, was thrown away, has come before this Board, since the change of flags, and applied for the lands: and such a case, if it were not for the "grant on absolute property," might we deem this of Merando's to be. If he had asked for ten leagues square of Governor White, and the Governor had said, "let it be done in proportion to his family," and Merando had proved that he had 1000 negroes or a thousand children, Merando would have been entitled to the amount, however large, which, by the regulations, he could claim for them; but, as he has proved neither the one nor the other, and has never surveyed the land, even if the grant be genuine, he can take nothing by a title like this.

No. 18.

F. M. Arredondo, *Claimant*—1,500 *acres of land.*

This is a part of a grant for 10,000 acres of land made to Entralgo, and recommended for confirmation by the Board of Land Commissioners.

No. 19.

Belton A. Copp, *Claimant*—1,500 *acres land.*

This is a part of a grant made to George Clarke, of 26,000 acres, already reported.

No. 20.

A. Gay, *Claimant—500 acres land.*

This is a part of a grant made to George Fleming, and reported in this abstract, No. 7.

No. 21.

Peter Meranda, *Claimant—2,000 acres land.*

This is a part of 10,000 acres, claimed by Meranda, and recommended to Congress for confirmation by the former Board of Land Commissioners.

A part of this same claim, 4,000 acres, has been sold to Juan B. Entralgo, and recommended by the same Board.

Jos. M. Hernandez, *Claimant.*

No. 22.	10,000 *acres land at*	*Salt Spring.*	
23.	5,000	"	*West side St. John's.*
24.	5 000	"	*East St. John's.*
25. Frs. P. Sanchez,	1,400	"	

These tracts are all claimed under the same title. On the 18th November, 1817, Joseph M. Hernandez, alleging, in his memorial to the Governor, "That his, the Governor's, power, for the distribution of land, is unlimited," for the several causes of "military services and an increased force on the part of the petitioner," prayed the donation of 20,000 acres of land, divided as above specified. The Governor alleges that, as the petitioner is one of those who contribute most to the improvement of the province, the land is granted in absolute property and dominion.

In 1820, on the application of Hernandez, Andrew Bergevin was authorized to survey the several tracts. He did so, and for this service Hernandez conveyed to him 1,400 acres, the same now claimed by F. P. Sanchez, No. 25.

If Hernandez is correct in his memorial, &c. "the power of the Governor to grant lands was unlimited," then this claim of 20,000 acres is good. But, as we entertain and have expressed a different opinion upon that subject, we cannot recommend the whole of it for confirmation.

No. 26.

Francis P. Sanchez, *Claimant—500 acres of land.*

This is a part of 10,000 acres granted to F. M. Arredondo, 5,000 acres of which, lying upon Back Creek, was sold to John B. Entralgo, in whose name that quantity was recommended by the former Board of Land Commissioners; and 4,000 acres of the same grant, lying east of Spring Garden, have been recommended in the name of the same individual. These three are parts of one integral grant, and cannot be severed in the decision.

No 27.

Henry Eckford, *Claimant—46,080 acres of land—Hillsboro' Bay.*

This is part of the land claimed by Pedro Miranda, No. 17 of this report.

No. 28.

JASPER WARD, *Claimant*—128,000 *acres of land.*

No. 29.

DIONISIA SEGUE, *Claimant*—5,333 *acres.*

No. 30.

DIONISIA SEGUE, *Claimant*—4,000 *acres.*

No. 31.

ANNE ORTEGA, *Claimant*—100 *acres.*

No. 32.

ANNE ORTEGA, *Claimant*—100 *acres.*

No. 32.

RALPH KING, *Claimant*—5,000 *acres.*

These claims are portions of large grants purchased of the grantees by the several claimants.

No. 28 is a moiety of a large Alachua grant, made to F. M. Arredondo & Son; which was recommended for confirmation by the Board of Land Commissioners.

No. 29 is a part of a Mill grant, made to Samuel Miles, and reported on by this Board during the session of 1827.

No. 30 is a part of a grant made to E. M. Gomez, and reported on above, No. 4.

No. 31 is a part of a large grant made to Peter Meranda; see this report No. 21.

No. 32 is part of a grant made to Antonio Huertas, which was recommended by the Board of Commissioners.

No. 33 is part of a Mill grant, claimed by F. Bethune, and reported on by this Board during the last session.

No. 34.

ANDREW BURGEVIN, *Claimant*—500 *acres of land.*

No. 35.

A. BURGEVIN, *Claimant*—500 *acres.*

No. 34 is situated on a branch, that runs from the West into the River St. John's, and is about 12 miles south of Lake George. It is a part of a larger grant, made to A. Huertas, and already reported on, by whom this tract was sold to the present claimant.

No. *35* is situated at a place called Big Spring, and is a portion of a large grant made to Peter Merando, and also reported on.

No. 36.

JACOB WORLDLY, *Claimant*—4 *miles square of land.*

This claim was filed here on the 12th November, 1828, and we regret that it was filed at all, as it is decidedly the most confounded claim that has ever been presented to us; it is a mill grant, all of which we thought we had decided on during the last year. On the 27th April, 1817, Jacob Worldly, representing himself to be desirous of building a water saw mill on Trout Creek, on the River St. John's, applied for a right of "four miles square, or its equivalent, for the necessary and contingent consumption of wood." On the 3d June, same year, the grant was made by Governor Coppinger, under the precise condition, "That, until the said machinery is erected, the concession shall be without effect:" and, further, "With the understanding, that, unless the construction of said machinery shall take place within the term of six months from the date hereof, the said grant shall be null and of no value."

This was in June, 1817; the claim, as we have said before, was filed in 1828, a term of more than eleven years. It is not proved or pretended that the machinery was erected within the six months prescribed by the grant, or at any subsequent period up to the present time, and yet it is claimed by Worldly. It is rejected.

No. 37.

THE HEIRS OF THOMAS FITCH—4,500 *acres of land.*

Governor Coppinger issues a Royal title, for four thousand five hundred acres of land, situated on the River Halifax, for services under the Royal order of the 29th March, 1815, to Fernando de la Maza Arredondo, Jun., which title is dated the 7th March, 1816. Thomas Fitch has purchased of Arredondo, and claims before this Board. It is considered a good claim, and we recommend it for confirmation.

No. 38.

DOMINGO FERNANDAS, *Claimant*—16,000 *acres of land.*

This claim is bad. It is supported by no other evidence than Aguilar's certificate, dated the 17th of November, 1817. It purports to have been granted for the many losses and services of the petitioner. The lands are located, by the petition itself, in Cabbage Swamp. We cannot recommend it for confirmation.

C. DOWNING,
W. H. ALLEN.

REPORT No. 3.—Register of Claims to Land exceeding 3,500

Numbers.	Names of		Date of patent, or royal title.	Date of concession, or order of survey.	Quantity of land.	By whom conceded.
	Present claimants.	Original claimants.			Acres.	
1	James Darley -	James Darley -	-	Nov. 10, 1817	23,000	Coppinger
2	Joseph Delispine -	Joseph Delispine -	-	April 9, 1817	43,000	Do
3	Do -	Pablo Fontaine -	-	1817	10,244	Do
4	Eusebio M. Gomez -	Eusebio M. Gomez	-	July 16, 1815	12,000	Do
5	Daniel O. Hara -	D. O. Hara -	-	Sept. 3, 1803	15,000	White, -
6	Philip R. Yonge -	P. R. Yonge -	1816,	- -	25,000	Coppinger
7	Heirs of Geo Fleming	George Fleming -	1816,	- -	20,000	Do
8	Antonio Acosta -	Antonio Acosta -	-	May, 1816	8,000	Do
9	Francis J. Avice -	Arredondo -	-	- -	500	-
10	Francisca Aguilar -	Francisco Aguilar -	-	Feb. 24, 1794	30,000	Quesada
11	George Atkinson, -	Geo. Atkinson -	-	Oct. 20, 1816	15,000	Coppinger
12	Do -	Peter Miranda -	-	Feb. 1810	4,000	White -
13	Francis M. Arredondo	Frs. M. Arredondo	-	- -	38,000	Coppinger
14	Do -	Do -	-	1810	50,000	White -
15	J. M. Arredondo -	J. M. Arredondo -	Jan. 12, 1811	- -	40,000	Do -
16	F. M. Arredondo -	F. M. Arredondo -	-	April 2, 1809	250,000	Do -
17	Peter Merando -	P. Merando -	-	Nov. 19, 1810	368,640	Do -
18	F. M. Arredondo -	Juan Etralgo -	-	- -	-	-
19	Belton A. Copp -	Geo. J. F. Clarke -	-	- -	1,500	-
20	A. Gay - -	Geo. Fleming -	-	- -	500	-
21	Peter Miranda -	Peter Miranda -	-	- -	2,000	-
22	Jos. M. Hernandez -	- -	-	- -	10,000	-
23	Do -	- -	-	- -	5,000	-
24	Do -	- -	-	- -	5,000	-
25	Francis P. Sanchez -	- -	-	- -	1,400	-
26	Frs. P. Sanchez -	F. M. Arredondo -	-	- -	500	-
27	Henry Eckford -	Peter Miranda -	-	- -	46,080	-

acres, which have been reported to Congress during the session, 1828.

Authority or royal order under which the concession was granted.	Date of survey.	By whom surveyed.	Situation.	General remarks.
-	Dec. 17, 1817	Geo. J. F. Clarke	Dunn's Lake, -	This is Tho. de Aguilar's certificate.
1815	-	- -	Indian River, -	Same as the above.
1815	-	And'w Burgevin	Trout Creek, -	Do do.
1815	-	- -	Rivers Jupiter and Santa Lucia,	Do do.
1790	-	- -	Between the rivers St. John's and St. Mary's,	Do do.
1815	-	- -	Spring Garden.	
1815	-	- -	Indian River.	
1815	-	Geo. J. F. Clarke	At different places. See Report.	Aguilar's certificate.
-	-	- -	- -	This is part of a grant for 30,000 acres, recommended for confirmation by the Board of Commissioners.
-	-	- -	Haw Creek, St. John's River,	This is Aguilar's certificate. See Report.
1815	-	- -	West side Upper Little Lake.	
1790	-	- -	See Report.	
1816	-	- -	Alligator Creek.	
1815				
1815	-	- -	Oquillabaga.	
-	-	- -	At a place called Calaso Gachey.	
1815	-	- -	Tampa Bay.	
-	-	- -	- -	This is a part of a grant of 10,000 acres, made to Entralgo, and recommended for confirmation by the Board of Commissioners.
-	-	- -	- -	A part of a grant made to Geo. J. F. Clarke, of 26,000 acres, and reported on during this session. Vide case. Report.
-	-	- -	- -	A part of No. 7 of this Abstract.
-	-	- -	- -	This is part of a grant of 10,000 acres made to Miranda, some portion of which has been recommended for confirmation by the former Commissioners.
-	-	- -	Salt Spring.	
-	-	- -	West side of St. Johns	These are subdivisions of a grant of 20,000 acres made to Jos. M. Hernandez, on 18th Nov. 1817.
-	-	- -	East side of St. Johns	
-	-	- -	A part of the above.	
-	-	- -	- -	This is a part of a grant of 10,000 acres made to F. M. Arredondo, the most of which has been recommended for confirmation by the Board of Commissioners.
-		- -	- -	This is a part of a larger grant to Peter Miranda, and reported on at length above, No. 17.

14

Numbers.	NAMES OF Present claimants.	NAMES OF Original claimants.	Date of patent, or royal title.	Date of concession, or order of survey.	QUANTITY OF LAND. Acres	By whom conceded.
28	Jasper Ward -	F. M. Arredondo & son	-	- -	128,000	-
29	Dionisia Segui -	Samuel Miles -	-	- -	5,333	-
30	Do -	E. M. Gomez -	-	- -	4,000	-
31	Anne Ortega -	Peter Miranda -	-	- -	100	-
32	Do -	Antonio Huertas -	-	- -	100	-
33	Ralph King -	F. Bethune -	-	- -	5,000	-
34	Andrew Burgevin -	Antonio Huertas -	-	- -	500	-
35	Do -	Peter Miranda -	-	- -	500	-
36	Jacob Worldly -	Jacob Worldly -	-	- -	4 m. sq.	-
37	The heirs of Th. Fitch	F. M. Arredondo, jr	Mar. 7, 1816	- -	4,500	-
38	Domingo Fernandez -	D. Fernandez -	-	- -	16,000	-

Continued.

Authority or royal order under which the concession was granted	Date of survey.	By whom surveyed.	Situation.	General remarks.
-	-	- -	- -	This is a moiety of the Alachua grant, which was recommended for confirmation.
-	-	- -	- -	Part of a mill grant, and reported by this Board during the session of 1827.
-	-	- -	- -	Part of a grant of 12,000 acres. See No. 4 of this Report.
-	-	- -	- -	Part of a larger grant. See this Report, No 21.
-	-	- -	- -	Part of a grant which was recommended by the Board of Commissioners.
-	-	- -	- -	Part of a mill grant to F. Bethune, and reported on by this Board during the last session.
-	-	- -	- -	Part of a large grant already reported on.
-	-	- -	- -	Part of a large grant also reported on.
-	-	- -	- -	This is a mill grant, situated on Trout Creek, River St. John's.
-	-	- -	- -	This land is situated on the river Halifax, granted under the order of 1815.
-		- -	- -	This grant purports to have been made for services.

C. DOWNING,
W. H. ALLEN.

REPORTS, NOS. 4, 5, 6, AND 7.

AND

Nos. 1, 2, 3, and 4, of Donation Claims.

No. 4.

DONATION CLAIMS—REPORT No. 1.

No. 1.

Andrew Pacety, *Claimant—640 acres.*

The land is situated on Armstrong Branch, 14 or 15 miles West of St. Augustine. Antonio Coneres and Antonio Ponce depose, that the claimant commenced his cultivation in 1818, and has continued it ever since. That he was then over twenty-one years of age; has a white family, two negroes, and a stock of cattle, and no claim derived from the Spanish or British Go-ment. Confirmed.

No. 2.

Eleanor Hogins, *Claimant—640 acres.*

Robert Hutchinson and Wm. Black swear to the cultivation from 1818 to the present time. Her husband is since dead, leaving herself a widow with one child and several negroes. Hutchinson says, the husband had a grant from the Spanish Government, but the land was found to be covered by an older grant and abandoned. The claim is confirmed to Mrs. Hogins.

No. 3.

The heirs of John Garcias, *Claimants—200 acres of land.*

John M. Bowden deposes to the cultivation of the land, from the year 1818, to the death of Garcias in 1822. The case is fully made out, with the exception of the quantity to which he is entitled; we think the quantity allowed is all that can be given under the deposition.

No. 4.

WM. SILCOX, *Claimant*—640 *acres*.

This land lies on Willis creek, near Cedar swamp, in the county of Duval, and on the St. John's river; two witnesses swear, that, in 1819, he was the head of a family, and 21 years of age, and lived on the tract claimed the whole of that year, and some time previous. We have no criterion by which to judge of the size of his family, but, as he appears to be an old settler, and the land is poor, we confirm to him the 640 acres of land.

No. 5.

JOHN EDGE, *Claimant*—640 *acres*.

Three witnesses prove that he is fairly entitled to the land claimed. It lies at the head of *Sawpit* branch, South of Julington creek. He settled it in 1818, with a large family, and has resided on it ever since. Confirmed.

No. 6.

JOHN CARR, *Claimant*—250 *acres*.

This land is situated on the South side of Lofton's swamp, emptying into Nassau river.

George Wilds proves cultivation from 1817 to the date of his affidavit, 1825; he proves all that is required by the statute. There is no evidence as to the size of his family, and 250 acres are confirmed.

No. 7.

JOHN DIXON, *Claimant*—350 *acres*.

This land is situated on St. Mary's river, on the public road. Two witnesses prove the claimant to have lived on the land twenty years. In one of his papers he claims 640 acres, in another 350. We confirm to him 350 acres.

No. 8.

REUBEN CHARLES, *Claimant*—350 *acres*.

This tract is about 12 miles North of St. Augustine, in the 12 mile swamp. George Gianoply deposes, "that, in 1818, he was upon the land claimed by Charles, who had a large log house on said land, and had three or four acres cleared; that in the year 1819, he planted rice," &c. Andrew Storrs was there in the year 1822, and found Charles and his family in possession. Wm.

Hartley and James Plummer prove his possession before 1819, and afterwards; that he was a married man, and fifty or sixty years old. Another witness proves that he has no land derived from the British or Spanish Government.

There is no witness to prove the number of his family, but, from all the circumstances, we think fit to give him 350 acres.

No. 9.

Bartolo Solana, *Claimant*—640 *acres.*

This land is situated near Big Cypress Swamp, and near the St. John's River. It is proved by one witness, that claimant settled this land in 1816, and has lived on it to the present time; that he has a large family, and a stock of one hundred head of cattle; and that he has no claim from the British or Spanish Government. It is confirmed.

No. 10.

Magdalena Solana, *Claimant*—640 *acres.*

This land is situated South side of Six Mile Creek, East of St. John's River.

Andres Papy and Bartolo Solana prove, "that, from 1818 to the present time, the claimant has possessed and cultivated the land." "She has a daughter and three negroes." We confirm to her this claim. Sometime after the 24th January, 1818, a grant was made to her deceased husband, of 1000 acres of land, which claim was barred by the treaty, and is therefore equivalent to no grant at all. If the Spanish Government thought fit to give her 1000 acres, we have no hesitation in confirming to her 640 acres.

No. 11.

Emanuel Crespo, *Claimant*—640 *acres.*

This land is said to be situated about a mile to the North of Tocoy Creek. near St. John's River.

It is in proof before the Board, that claimant has been in continued possession of the land, with a numerous family, from the year 1818 to the present time, and every way entitled to the land. It is confirmed.

No. 12.

Robert Miller, *Claimant*—200 *acres of land.*

Many witnesses have deposed to the fact, that James Baird, in the first instance, and afterwards the present claimant, who intermarried with Baird's widow after his death, cultivated a place called Martin's Island, from the year 1814 to 1822. The island is supposed to contain about 200 acres, and as the evidence is perfect, the claim is confirmed.

C. DOWNING.
W. H. ALLEN.

ABSTRACT No. 4.

Donation Claims which have been confirmed by the Register and Receiver for East Florida, during the Session of 1828.

nants.	Quantity.	Situation.	General Remarks.
	Acres.		
- -	640	14 or 15 miles West of St. Augustine	
- -	640	Pottsburgh creek, St. John's river	
Garcias -	200	One mile from St. John's river	
- -	640	Willis's creek, Cedar swamp	
- -	640	Head of Sawpit branch, South of Julington	
- -	250	South side Loftin's Swamp, Nassau river	
- -	350	St. Mary's river, on the public road	
- -	350	12 miles North of St. Augustine, 12 mile swamp	
- -	640	Near Big Cypress swamp, St. John's river	
- -	640	South of 6 mile creek, East of St. John's river	
- -	640	North of Tocoy creek, near St. John's river	
- -	200	Martin's Island	

C. DOWNING.
W. H. ALLEN.

No. 5.

DONATION CLAIMS—REPORT No. 2.

No. 1.

John Jones, *Claimant—640 acres of land.*

John Jones has two claims before the Board, derived from Spanish grants; one for 100 acres, has been confirmed—the other, for 500, has been rejected. It may or may not be the same individual, though we are inclined to believe it is. Five or six witnesses testify that Jones never settled upon this land until August, 1823.—This claim is rejected.

No. 2.

John B. Strong, *Claimant—640 acres of land.*

This claim is supported by no evidence; and it is a matter of notoriety. that he never lived in the country.—Rejected.

No. 3.

Henry Swinney, *Claimant—640 acres of land.*

There is no evidence in this claim, and we reject it.

No. 4.

Abraham Bellamy, *Claimant—640 acres of land.*

There is no evidence, and the claim is rejected.

No. 5.

William Haddock, *Claimant—640 acres of land.*

No evidence.—Rejected.

No. 6.

Thomas Jones, *Claimant—640 acres of land.*

There is no evidence, and it is rejected

No. 7.

William Hart, *Claimant*—640 *acres of land.*

This land is situated on the West side of St. John's river, on Trout and Moncriff's Creeks.

This claim is rejected, for two reasons: *First,* That four witnesses are sworn, that William Hart lived upon the land, improved, and cultivated the same in 1810 or 1812.

They further add that he and his heirs had possession of the land ever since. From this testimony it is evident that the possession spoken of is what the deponents consider a legal possession. The law of 1824 requires, that, on the 22d February, 1819, the claimant should have actually inhabited and cultivated the tract. This does not appear by the testimony to be the case.

Secondly. William Hart, by his representatives, has presented to this Board a claim for 1400 acres of land, derived from the Spanish Government. No. 42, Report 2.

No. 8.

James Burney, *Claimant*—640 *acres of land.*

This land is situated on the South side of Trout Creek, near the mouth of Six Mile Creek.

From the testimony of Robert Rawlins and Benjamin Rawlins, it appears that the claimant lived upon this land from the year 1818 to 1820, but it no where appears that he was then 21 years of age, or the head of a family, or that he had any claim derived from the Spanish or British Government.

It should, moreover, be added, that this claim was filed in this office on the 3d October of the present year. And we are under the impression, that the period allowed to parties to file their claims, which, by the law of 1827, expired on the 1st November of that year, was not revived by the law of 1828. For these reasons this claim is rejected.

No. 9.

John Ashton, *Claimant*—640 *acres of land.*

This land lies about a mile from Mr. Cowen's, and 12 miles from St. John's river.

Joseph Somerall swears, that the claimant was driven off of the place in 1812, by the dangers of the revolution. That he was a single man, and upwards of twenty-one years of age.

The law requires the party to live upon the land in 1819, which he did not; that he should be the head of a family, which a single man without slaves is not; that he should have no claim derived from the Spanish Government; and Ashton has filed the certificate of survey of George Clarke, for 300 acres, dated 10th April, 1818. For all these reasons, and because the claim was never filed until November, 1828, it is rejected.

No. 10.

Manuel Solana, *Claimant*—640 *acres of land.*

This land is described to be "eight miles South of Picolata Fort, on the St. John's River.

There are three depositions in this case:

1st. John Andrew, who says, "in 1817 or 1818, on a place near M'Cullock's branch, the claimant resided and had some cattle;" "that he had a person living on said land who cultivated a part of it." Andrew afterwards stated to the Receiver, Mr. Allen, that he had been mistaken as to the property, and knew nothing of the matter.

2d. Manuel Crespo deposes, that he is acquainted with claimant, who took possession of this tract in 1819, and built houses thereon; and he does not know that claimant owns any other lands in the Territory.

3d. C. W. Clarke swears that he knows the claimant, whom he considers as a head of a family.

This claim is rejected: 1st. because it does not appear, from the deposition of Crespo, that Solana was in possession of the land on the 22d day of February, 1819.

2dly, Mr. Solana is a single man, without property, and whatever Mr. Clark may think, cannot be considered as the head of a family.

No. 11.

John Toy, *Claimant*—640 *acres of land.*

No. 12.

Francis Durant, *Claimant*—640 *acres.*

No. 13.

Joseph Watson, *Claimant*—640 *acres.*

No. 14.

Richard D. Ford, *Claimant*—640 *acres.*

No. 15.

Peter Nicholas, *Claimant*—640 *acres.*

No. 16.

NATHANIEL TANNER, *Claimant*—640 *acres*.

No. 17.

JESSE WILSON, *Claimant*—640 *acres*.

No. 18.

BLAKE WILLIAMSON, *Claimant*—640 *acres*.

No. 19.

ROBERT GILBERT, *Claimant*—232 *acres*.

No. 20.

JOSEPH R. PREVAT, *Claimant*—640 *acres*.

No. 21.

RICHARD TICE, *Claimant*—640 *acres*.

No. 22.

ANN STALLING, *Claimant*—640 *acres*.

No. 23.

JOHN BELLAMY, *Claimant*—640 *acres*.

No. 24.

THOMAS PREVAT—*Claimant*—640 *acres*.

No. 25.

JOHN BELLAMY, *Claimant*—150 *acres*.

No. 26.

William Williamson, *Claimant*—640 *acres*.

In these cases, from No. 11 to 26, inclusive, there is no evidence whatever; and they are all rejected.

No. 27.

William Gardner, *Claimant*—640 *acres*.

This land is situated near the St. John's river.

Two witnesses swear that claimant "*never took no head rights*," except 150 acres on Julington creek. His taking this 150 acres is fatal to his donation claim. Rejected.

No. 28.

Nathaniel Stephens, *Claimant*—640 *acres*.

This land lies on the Little St. Mary's river.

The evidence in this case proves that, in 1818, the claimant lived upon the land, with a wife and two children. Bailey, the witness, was at his residence in 1818; and whether he remained there until the 22d February, 1819, does not appear. Wherefore, it is rejected.

No. 29.

Benjamin Rawlins, *Claimant*—640 *acres*.

Rawlins claims the land lying in the county of Alachua, on San Filasko creek. The testimony produced clashes with his claim. John Uptegrove, the only witness sworn, deposes, in 1825, "that he, claimant, had resided on a place called Bear Branch, Nassau Creek, Duval county, from the year 1818 to that time. We cannot confirm to him the place on Bear Branch, for he does not claim it; nor the place on Alachua, for he does not prove his claim. And they are widely apart.

No. 30.

Emanuel D. Mott, *Claimant*—640 *acres*.

The land lies on the River St. John's.

Samuel Fairbanks and John Jones both swear that the claimant settled on the land about two years before the 8th day of December, 1824, the date of their deposition. This carries the settlement back to the 8th December, 1822; and the claim must, of course, be rejected.

No. 31.

JOHN ANDREW, *Claimant*—640 *acres.*

B. Solana deposes, that, two years previous to the exchange of flags, claimant took possession of the land, planted potatoes and pumpkins, kept stock, and had cow pens; built a house when he took possession, which blew down in 1825; and continued in possession until September of the same year. When cross-examined, he says that Mr. Andrew had no negroes, never resided on the land for five or six months at a time; and was not, when he took possession, a married man, or the head of a family. It is rejected.

No. 32.

DAVID WILLIAMSON, *Claimant*—640 *acres.*

This land is claimed in Alachua. There is no evidence filed in the case; and Horatio Dexter has sworn, in another case, that there were no settlements in Alachua previous to the change of flags; which we believe to be the fact. This claim is rejected.

No. 33.

WILLIAM DANIEL, *Claimant*—640 *acres.*

This land is situated on St. Mary's river, on Deep Run creek. Two witnesses prove, that, on the 22d February, 1819, he inhabited and cultivated the land, "and has had principal control of his father's family, before and after the date above mentioned."

From this evidence, it is plain that Daniel was a young man, living with his father, and managing his estate. We do not consider his case as embraced by the law, and reject it.

No. 34.

THOMAS BOWDEN, *Claimant*—640 *acres.*

Two witnesses have deposed, "that, when they knew Thomas Bowden, (without saying at what time) he lived on a certain tract of land on the South side of Goodsby's lake, said to contain 250 acres, and cultivated the same for many years."

This evidence is not sufficient to support the claim, and it is rejected.

No. 35.

JOSEPH AND MATTHEW LONG, *Claimants*—640 *acres.*

This land is said to be situated on Graham's creek, near the King's road. Gab. W. Perpall and Charles W. Clark say, that the parents of the claimants took possession of the land in 1800, abandoned it in 1812, reclaimed their possession before 1824; and the present claimants, now above twenty-one years of age, have had possession of it since 1822 or 1823.

This claim must be rejected, because the Longs have two claims filed before this Board, No. , Report , derived by grants from the Spanish Government.

The case is plain enough. The Longs had a grant from the Spanish Government, which, it will be seen, they have neglected to produce, as they hoped to obtain a larger amount, under the Donation Law; and thus they have lost both of their claims.*

No. 36.

Heirs of Zachariah Haddock, *Claimant*—640 *acres.*

This land is situated on Cabbage swamp, St. Mary's river.

J. D. Hart deposes, that, in 1817, he was upon the land claimed; that it was then cultivated by Haddock, with two or three houses built upon it; that he was the head of a family, which consisted of a wife and two children, and was over the age of twenty-one. There was no evidence to prove that he continued his possession until 1819; and therefore it is rejected.

No. 37.

Gamaliel Darling, *Claimant*—640 *acres of land.*

John Leornardy, the only witness sworn in this case, says, that he, the witness, was upon the land in 1817; that Darling then had at work six hands: there was a small house, and some corn; the land lies in Twelve Mile swamp. No evidence is produced to show that the claimant lived upon the land in 1819, 1820, or 1821. It is therefore rejected.

C. DOWNING,
W. H. ALLEN.

* Since writing the above, the Longs have produced their titles, and their claim has been confirmed. See Report 1, No. 77.

ABSTRACT No. 5.

nation Claims which have been rejected by the Register and Receiver for East Florida, during the session of 1828.

ants.	Quantity. Acres.	Situation.	General Remarks.
- -	640	East bank St. John's River.	
- -	640	St. John's River - - -	No evidence.
- -	640	West side St. John's, Duval county.	
- -	640	Head of Thomas Swamp - -	Same.
- -	640	St. Mary's River, Nassau county -	Same.
- -	640	County of Alachua - - -	Same.
- -	640	W. side St. John's River, Trout Creek.	
- -	640	S. side Trout Creek, near Six Mile Cr.	
- -	640	12 miles from St. John's River.	
- -	640	8 miles South of Picolata, St. John's.	
- -	640	Alachua county.	
- -	640	Alachua.	
- -	640	North side Six Mile Creek.	
- -	640	Alachua.	
- -	640	Alachua.	
- -	640	Alachua.	
- -	640	Cedar Creek, St. John's River -	Two depositions brought in after 1st December, 1828.
- -	640	Nassau River, Duval County.	
- -	232	St. John's River.	
- -	640	St. Mary's River.	

ABSTRACT No. 5—Continued.

laimants.	Quantity. Acres.	Situation.	General Remarks.
	640	Cape Florida.	
	640	Goodby's Lake.	
	640	Cedar Creek.	See No. 25, following.
	640	St Mary's River, Nassau county.	
	150	South side M'Girt's Creek	Claimant first filed his petition for 640 acres, (No. 23, above,) and afterwards altered that quantity to 500 acres, and filed the present claim at another place, to complete his complement.
amson	640	-	This claim was rejected by old Board.
er	640	St. John's River.	
aens	640	St. Mary's River.	
ins	640	Sanfelasko Creek, Alachua.	
ott	640	River St. John's.	
	640	Tocoy Creek.	
son	640	Alachua.	
	640	Deep Run Creek, St. Mary's River.	
en	640	South side Goodby's Lake.	
hew Long	640	Graham's Creek, near King's Road.	
riah Haddock	640	Cabbage Swamp, St. Mary's River.	
ng	640	Twelve Mile Swamp.	

C. DOWNING,
W. H. ALLEN.

No. 6.

DONATION CLAIMS.—REPORT No. 3.

No. 1.

ADAM COOPER, *Claimant—640 acres of land.*

In a letter of the claimant, filed before this Board, he states, "that he lives on this land now, and has done so ever since 1822." He says, further, "that his claim was filed in October, 1827;" of this we have no recollection, nor is it so recorded. The affidavit of Benjamin Wood states positively, that claimant lived on the land situated in Little St. Mary's Neck, on the 22d February, 1819. This is at variance with the declaration in the letter; and we are more disposed to believe the man's word than his witnesses. The letter and affidavit are both dated in October, 1828, and filed on the 29th of the following month. Claim is rejected.

No. 2.

JOSEPH MARIA CALDEZ, *Claimant—640 acres of land.*

Maximo Hernandez deposes, that he has known the claimant about ten years; that he has occupied the land ever since he knew him; that he is over twenty-one years of age, a resident of Florida, the head of a family; has had possession of the land up to this time; and, as far as he believes, owns no land derived from the Spanish or British Government.

Domingo Alberes deposes, that he is acquainted with claimant, who settled the place in January, 1819. That he is now the head of a family, consisting of a wife and three children. From what we can gather from the papers, this land lies at a place called Angola, on Oyster River, near the Gulf of Mexico.

The testimony does not show, that in 1819 the claimant was 21 years of age, or a married man; and from the silence of the two affidavits upon that subject, and from their never failing to state those two important facts when they do exist, we are compelled to infer that Caldez is not embraced within the spirit or letter of the law of 1824. Above all, this claim was filed here in September, 1828, and is rejected.

No. 3.

ANTONIO MACHACO, *Claimant—640 acres.*

This land lies at Key Peublo, on the Gulf of Mexico, about eight or ten miles from Charlotte harbor.

Joseph Cadao swears, that he has known claimant 20 years, who has occupied the land claimed about 15 years (the deposition is dated in 1828;) that he is over the age of 21, a resident of *Florida*, the head of a family, claims no title from the British or Spanish Government, and has been in the actual possession of the land since 1813.

Regregrio Andres "has known claimant 15 or 20 years, who has cultivated the land claimed in 1819, and has a wife and one child."

The evidence in this case, as in the preceding, is defective. The claimant is not shown to have been an adult or married man in 1819: and, from having now but one child in a prolific country, we presume he was not married at that time. This claim was filed in September, 1828. It is rejected.

No. 4.

ANDREW GOZALES, *Claimant*—640 *acres.*

This land is situated on the Gulf side of Florida, on the Northeastern end of Sarasota Bay.

Joseph Caldo swears, "that he knows the claimant, who has resided on the land about 20 years; is fifty years of age, and the head of a family: that he has no land but this, and still lives upon it.

John Russel was on the place in 1824, where he found houses built, and provisions growing.

Housa Maria Pancia swears to nearly the same facts as Caldez. He says the claimant cultivated the land since 1819, and during that year: and that he has a wife and four children now living on the place. This claim was filed the 5th September, 1828.

No. 5.

ANTONIO GOMEZ, *Claimant*—640 *acres.*

This land lies on Sarasota Bay. The evidence in support of the claim is this: Joseph Caldez, in June, 1828, deposes, that he has known the claimant 20 years; who has lived upon the land 16 years, and is over the age of 21 years, a resident of Florida, the head of a family; has been in actual possession of the land up to the present time; and, as far as the witness knows, has neither Spanish or British grant.

Housa Maria Pancia "has known the claimant 10 years, who was in actual possession and cultivation of the land in 1819; he has planted fruit trees—he still lives on the place, and has a wife and five children." It will be observed, that none of the witnesses proved the party to have been 21 years of age or a married man in 1819, without which, his claim cannot be confirmed.

No. 6.

Julian George, *Claimant*—640 *acres.*

This land is described to be on Key Pelew, in the vicinity of Charlotte harbor. Jos. Maria Pancia, being sworn before a Justice of the Peace, deposes, "that he has known the claimant several years; that in 1819, he cultivated about 10 acres in corn and other provisions, and has now a wife and four children." The testimony of Jos. Caldez, is, that he has known the claimant, who has lived on the land 12 years, up to this date, he is 45 years of age, the head of a family, a resident of Florida, and has no claim derived from the Spanish or British Government. This claim is defective in proof as the preceding. It was filed on the 15th September, 1828.

No. 7.

Peruko Pompon, *Claimant*—640 *acres.*

This land is situated on Key Pelew, near Charlotte harbor. Domingo Alverez and Joseph Caldez testify, that they have known the claimant for about 12 years, and that he has resided on the place from that time to the present, (June, 1828;) that he is 40 years old, and the head of a family, consisting of a wife and three children, a resident of Florida; he claims no land derived from the British or Spanish Government. This claim was filed in September, 1828. It is equally defective with the cases immediately preceding, and is rejected.

No. 8.

Antonio Pancia, *Claimant*—640 *acres.*

We cannot discover whether this man's name is Pania or Pancia: he is the same who, as a witness, has been so often called in this report by the name of Pancia. The land which he claims lies on Key Pelew, about 8 miles North of Charlotte harbor.

Manual Hosa and Maximo Hernandez swear, that they have known the party about 12 or 15 years, that he has cultivated the place about 12 years, and that in 1819, he made a crop of corn and peas; that he has a wife and two children, the eldest of whom is about 10 years of age; that he has been in the actual possession of the place ever since, and, as far as the witnesses know, has no claim derived from the Spanish or British Government. This claim was filed in September, 1828.

No. 9.

Jos. Maria Godoya, *Claimant*—640 *acres.*

Maximo Hernandez, is the only witness sworn in this case, and his evidence has been so informally taken, that we cannot receive it. A commission in 1825, signed by the Secretary of the Board of Land Commissioners, and directed to two gentlemen, has been executed by one alone, and that one signs as a witness to the mark of Hernandez, and not as a Commissioner.

We will briefly state the evidence, such as it is. Witness knows the claimant, who has resided on the land, situated on Sarasota Bay, since the year 1812, to the date of the deposition, which, by the way, has no date; he is the head of a family, and *now*, over 21 years of age, and he believes claims no land derived from the British or Spanish Government. This claim was filed in September, 1828. Rejected.

No. 10.

JACOB YELVINGTON, *Claimant*—640 *acres.*

This land is situated on the South side of 6 mile Creek.

John Ford, the only witness sworn, says, that, at the date of his deposition, 17th October, 1828, the claimant was 21 years of age, and the head of a family; that he took possession of the land in January, 1821, and has resided on it ever since, either in person or by representative; that he had 5 or 6 in family, and that he believes, he has no claim derived from the Spanish or British Government.

We cannot recommend this claim, because it does not appear that claimant was a married man, or 21 years of age before the 17th July, 1821, and because this claim was filed in this office, after 1st November, 1827.

No. 11.

SARAH BALLARD, *Claimant*—640 *acres.*

James Burney and James Long, in October, 1828, depose, "that claimant lived on, and cultivated a tract of land, on the North side of Trout creek, at a place formerly called Carters, from the first of the year 1819, as early as February, to some time in 1820. Claimant is 21 years of age, and the head of a family. Witnesses do not believe she has any claim under the Spanish or British Government.

It appears from this evidence, that the claimant, at best, lived upon this land but a single year.

This claim was filed before this Board, in the month of October, 1828. We cannot confirm it.

No. 12.

FRANCIS J. AVICE, *Claimant*—640 *acres.*

The land is described, as "situated on the East side of St. John's river, between the lands of John B. Entralgo, and Dr. Brush, nearly opposite Paliattia."

Peter Rodriguez, swears, that he was on the land claimed previous to the exchange of flags, in the year 1821, and saw claimant at that time, who was building a house; and that there was also a family by the name of Stafford residing there. Witness believes the claimant was above the age of 21 at that time, and has no claim derived from the Spanish or British Government.

Mr Avice, at this time, has no lands immediately derived from either of those Governments, but he has large claims by purchase, which have been filed before this Board, and we therefore do not consider that his case is embraced by the spirit of the law. He was at that time a single man, and as such, we do not consider him as the head of a family.

If the testimony proves the title in any one, it is in Stafford, and not in Avice. The claim was filed in the year 1828, and we cannot recommend it.

No. 13.

SHEDDRICK STANLEY, *Claimant—640 acres.*

This would have been a good claim had it been filed sooner. It was presented here in October, 1828. The evidence is this: That claimant occupied the land on St. Mary's river, in the year 1800, and continued there until the year 1281; that he was then 21 years of age, and the head of a family, consisting of a number of children, and 3 or 4 negroes. The witnesses, J. D. Hart, and John Warren, never heard of his claiming any land under the Spanish or British Government.

No. 14.

JOAQUIN CALDEZ, *Claimant—640 acres.*

The land is situated on Oyster river, about 8 miles from Tampa bay.

Andrew Gomez and Antonia Frasia, say, that they have known claimant 15 years; that he is over the age of 21: that he is the head of a family, consisting of a wife and three children; has lived on the land ever since they knew him, and has no claim derived from the British or Spanish Government.

The evidence is defective in not proving that he was 21 years of age, and a married man, in 1819. The claim was filed in September, 1828, and is rejected.

No. 15.

DAVID HAGENS, *Claimant—640 acres of land.*

This land lies on the public road leading from Jacksonville to Camp Pinckney, in the fork of Mills Swamp, near the mouth of Alligator Creek, in the county of Nassau.

James Long, Benjamin Rawlins, and I. D. Hart, depose, that claimant settled on the land in 1817, and has resided there ever since, with a family of four children, and two or three negroes. That he was more than twenty-one years of age at the time, and has no claim derived from the Spanish or British Government.

If this claim had been filed sooner, it would be good ; but as it was never presented until October, 1828, if our view of the law be correct, we cannot confirm it.

No. 16.

JOHN HALL, *Claimant*—640 *acres of land.*

This land is described as lying on or near Cedar creek, on the West side of St. John's river. The evidence is, that, in February, 1819, he was the head of a family, twenty-one years of age, and settled on the land.

He is an old man, and if his claim had been filed in time, we would confirm it ; but it was presented to this Board in September, 1828.

No. 17.

JOHN SILCOX, *Claimant*—640 *acres of land.*

The witness proves that he actually lived on, and cultivated a tract of land on Cedar creek, on the West side of St John's river, during the whole of the year 1819, and before and after; that he was then twenty-one years of age, and the head of a family. This claim has been filed since the 1st of December, 1828, and must, of course, be rejected.

C. DOWNING,
W. H. ALLEN.

ABSTRACT No. 6.

REPORT No. 3, *of Donation Claims, Session of* 1828.

nts.	Age.	Quantity. Acres.	Situation.	Occupation or cultivation. from	to	General Remarks.
- -		640	Little St. Mary's river			
- -		640	Angola, Oyster river			
- -		640	Key Pueblo, Gulf of Mexico,			
- -		640	Sarrasota bay			
- -		640	Sarrasota bay			
- -		640	Key Peleu			
- -		640	Key Peleu			
- -		640	Key Peleu			
- -		640	Sarrasota bay			
- -		640	Six Mile creek			
- -		640	Trout creek			
- -		640	St. John river			
- -		640	St. Mary's river			
- -		640	Oyster river, near Tampa			
- -		640	Mills' swamp			
- -		640	Cedar creek, west of St. Johns			
-		640	Cedar creek, west of St. Johns			

C. DOWNING.
W. H. ALLEN.

No. 7.

DONATION CLAIMS.—REPORT No. 4.

No. 1.

JOHN F. BROWN, *Claimant*—640 *acres.*

The evidence in this case is this: First, the affidavit of the claimant, that, on the 19th July, 1819, and ever since that time, he has been in the possession and cultivation of a tract of land in Duval county, situated on the St. John's River, between Dunn's Creek and Clapboard Creek; that he was then 21 years of age, and the head of a family, and has no claim derived from the Spanish or British Government.

The facts just stated from claimant's affidavit, are fully proved by two respectable witnesses.

Mr. Brown is a man of a large family, and we recommend this claim to Congress for confirmation.

No. 2.

JAMES ROWSE, *Claimant*—640 *acres.*

This land is situated on St. Mary's river. The claimant settled the place in 1819, during the month of March, and, by the evidence produced, he is entitled to the land. We therefore recommend it for confirmation.

No. 3.

COTTON ROWLES, *Claimant*—640 *acres.*

Three witnesses have deposed that this land, situated on the South prong, and near the head of Trout Creek, was settled by the claimant about the beginning of the year 1821, and that he resided on it until 1823 or '24. They further prove, that he is the head of a family, and over 21 years of age, and has no land derived from the Spanish or British Government. We recommend his claim for confirmation.

No. 4.

WADE SILCOX, *Claimant*—640 *acres.*

This land is situated on the head of Thomas' Swamp, near the line of Nassau and Duval counties. The testimony of two witnesses is, that the claimant settled on the land in 1820, and has remained in possession of, and cultivated it, ever since; that he was then over 21 years of age, the head of a family, consisting of a wife and child, and claimed no lands derived from the British or Spanish Government.

This claim was filed here in the month of November, 1828, and it will be seen by reference to report No. 3, donation claims, that the Board have not considered themselves authorized by law, to confirm claims filed subsequently to the 1st November, 1827. But as these cases, the cultivation of which commenced between February, 1819, and July, 1821, are of necessity to be reported to Congress, we feel it our duty to say, that, had this case been filed in time, we should not have hesitated to recommend it for confirmation.

C. DOWNING,
W. H. ALLEN.

ABSTRACT No. 7.

onation Claims founded on Habitation and Cultivation, commenced between the 22*d February,* 1819, *and the* 17*th July*, 1821, *and recommended for confirmation.*

nts.	Quantity. Acres.	Situation.	General Remarks.
-	640	East of St. John's river	
-	640	St. Mary's river	
-	640	Head of Trout creek, St. John's	
	640	Thomas's Swamp	

C. DOWNING,
W. H. ALLEN.

REPORT No. 8. OF BRITISH CLAIMS.

No. 1.	WILLIAM TRAVERS.	500	Acres
2.	Same.	500	"
3.	Same.	500	"
4.	Same.	500	"
5.	Same.	500	"
6.	Same.	750	"
7.	Same.	500	"
8.	Same.	500	"
9.	Same.	2,000	"
10.	Same.	500	"

In these cases, William Travers claims, as agent, No. 1, 2, 3, 4, 5, and 6, for the heirs of Thomas Forbes; No. 7, 8, 9, and 10, for the heirs of William Panton.

It is a matter of public notoriety, that the house of Panton, Leslie & Forbes, of which Thomas Forbes and William Panton were partners, continued by the permission of the Spanish Government to do a large mercantile business in the city of St. Augustine, and were generally employed by the Government to furnish supplies, both in money and in goods.

Some of the partners of this house were permitted to purchase lands and to hold them in East Florida; it has not appeared to us that either of the above claimants, Forbes or Panton, took the oath of allegiance to the Spanish Government, or became Spanish subjects. The only evidence which has been produced to us, is a certificate from the keeper of the public archives of this city, that Don John Leslie, as appears by some of the records in his office, presented himself for the house of Panton, Leslie, & Co. and declared the four principals of the house to be William Panton and Thomas Forbes, (the present claimants) Charles Maclatchy and himself, and that the said company owned in this province 72,820 acres of land.

By the regulations of Government here, the British subjects holding lands were required to present themselves to the proper authorities, and to make known the number of acres claimed by them, and the course they intended to adopt: that is to say, they were required to declare whether their intention was to sell their lands and retire, or to become Spanish subjects and remain.

The claimants in these cases have so presented themselves, and have declared themselves owners of the above quantity of land. It is more than probable that they performed the other requisites of the law, but from the little care with which the records of that time were preserved, it is more than probable that the evidence of that fact has been lost. Suffice it to say, that as Panton and Forbes remained in the province during the whole time of the Spanish dominion, presented themselves to the Government as the owners of these lands, were accredited and favored agents and owners of lands other than these, we are disposed to believe these claims are good.

The position of the land, together with the date of the grant, and the Governor who made it, may be seen by reference to the abstract accompanying this report.

No. 11.	FRANCIS KINLOCK.	2,350 *Acres.*
12.	Same.	500 "
13.	Same.	500 "

The date of the grants and the locality of these several tracts, will appear upon the abstract accompanying this report.

These are marked British grants, unaccompanied by any proof that these claims were ever recognised by the Spanish Government. Indeed it is not so pretended. The Kinlocks were, by their own shewing, always British subjects or American citizens; and we presume there can be no question of the position, that all such claims are bad.

C. DOWNING, *Register.*
W. H. ALLEN, *Receiver.*

REPORT No. 8.

ABSTRACT of British Grants reported during the Session of 1828.

nts.	Original Claimants.	Acres.	Date of Grant.	Governor.	Situation of the Land.
s, agt.	Thomas Forbes	500	15 Feb. 1781	Tonyn	Cedar Swamp, St. John's river
	same	500	11 Nov. 1782	same	Lake Lomond, St. John's river
	same	500	3 Feb. 1780	same	Lake George
	same	500	same	same	Spring Creek, Lomond Grove
	same	500	16 June, 1782	same	Cedar Swamp, near river St. John's
	same	750	11 Nov. 1782	same	St. John's river, near Hester's Bluff
	William Panton	500	3 Feb. 1780	same	Spring Creek, part Lomond Grove
	same	500	3 May, 1782	same	Cedar Swamp Landing
	same	2,000	16 June, 1782	same	Cedar Swamp
	same	500	15 Feb. 1781	same	Cedar Swamp, west St. John's riv.
k, jun.	Francis Kinlock, sen.	2,350	3 June, 1776	Grant	On the east side of St. John's river
	same	500	3 June, 1766	same	East side of St. John's river
	same	500	1766	same	St. John's river

C. DOWNING,
W. H. ALLEN.

REPORT No. 9.

REGISTER OF CLAIMS TO TOWN LOTS WHICH HAVE BEEN CONFIRMED.

REGISTER of Claims to Town Lots which have been Con

Numbers.	Names of Present Claimants.	Names of Original Claimants.	Date of Patent or Royal Title.	Date of concession or order of survey.	Quantity of Land.	
					No. of lot.	Acres and 100dths.
1	Bernardo Segui	Bernardo Segui	-	-	3&4sq. 19	578 sq. ft.
2	Heirs of Jas. Cashen	Manuel Rengil	-	16 Dec. 1809	-	A lot
3	The heirs of John D. Kehr	John D. Kehr	-	15 Feb. 1811	-	A lot
4	The heirs of James Cashen	James Cashen	10 Apr 1817	-	3 sq. 1	A lot
5	Same	Same	-	9 Jan. 1810	-	A lot
6	Arbena Fallis	A Fallis	24 Dec. 1814	-	4&5sq. 22	2 half lots
7	Geronimo Alvarez	G. Alvarez	26 Mar. 1818	-	7	A lot
8	Same	Same	26 Mar 1818	-	13&14 s 9	2 half lots
9	Maria Mills	William Mills	19 Dec. 1818	-	12 sq. 17	A lot
10	Domingo Rodriguez	D. Rodriguez	-	26 May, 1819	6 13	A lot
11	Maria R. Scott	Maria R Scott	-	13 Mar. 1811	8 16	A lot
12	Farquhar Bethune	Samuel Harrison	15 Sept. 1814	-	10 4	A lot
13	Bethune & Sibbald	Bethune & Sibbald	-	26 Sept. 1815	-	Marsh lot
14	F. M. Arredondo, jr	F. M Arredondo, jr	-	7 Mar. 1812	-	A lot
15	The heirs of J. Alexander	Be de Castro y Ferrer	-	-	-	7
16	The heirs of Josiah Smith	Dn Travers	-	-	-	40824 s. y.
17	Joseph F. White	Eusebius Bushnel	-	-	2undvd. $\frac{1}{3}$	A lot
18	The heirs of C. B. Bulow	Maria C. Miranda	-	-	A house	and lot
19	Same	Matias Pons	9 April, 1813	-	-	6
20	Robert Mitchell	Dn. Bosquet	-	-	-	13 9.100
21	F. B. Gould	F M. Arredondo	-	2 May, 1807	-	A lot

In these cases, the titles are good. We do not deem it necessary to are all confirmed.

No. 9.

firmed by the Register and Receiver, during the Session of 1828.

By whom conceded.	Conditions.	Date of survey.	By whom surveyed.	Situation.	Numbers.
Coppinger -	Complied with	10 May, 1814	George J. F. Clarke	Fernandina -	1
White -	do do	- -	- - -	Same -	2
White -	do do	- -	- - -	Same -	3
Coppinger -	do do	2 Jan. 1817	George J. Clarke -	Same -	4
White -	do do	- -	-	Same -	5
Kindelan -	do do	10 Nov. 1814	George J. F. Clarke	Same -	6
Coppinger -	do do	10 June, 1817	George J. F. Clarke	Same -	7
Coppinger -	do do	10 June, 1817	George J. F. Clarke	Same -	8
Coppinger -	do do	10 June, 1816	George J. F. Clarke	Same -	9
Coppinger -	do do	12 Feb. 1817	George J. F. Clarke	Same -	10
White -	do do	15 May, 1817	George J. F. Clarke	Same -	11
Kindelan -	do do	7 Sept. 1814	George J. F. Clarke	Same -	12
Estrada -	- -	- -	- - -	Same -	13
Estrada -	do do	-	- - -	St. Augustine	14
- -	do do	2 Nov. 1819	Andrew Burgevin -	St. Augustine	15
- -	.. -	9 Dec. 1819	Andrew Burgevin -	St. Augustine	16
- -	- -	- -	- - -	St. Augustine	17
- -	- -	- -	- - -	St Augustine	18
Kindelan -	- -	23 May, 1821	Andrew Burgevin -	St. Augustine	19
- -	- -	- -	- - -	St Augustine	20
White -	- -	- -	- - -	St. Augustine	21

make a special report in each case, nor have we time, if so disposed. They

C. DOWNING,
W. H. ALLEN

No. 10.

A LIST of Claims to Town Lots in which no title and no evidence has been filed or produced.

No.	Claimants.	Quantity.	City or Town in which the Lots are situated.	Remarks.
1	R. Mitchell, &c. ass. -	2 lots	Fernandina	
2	Assr. Carrachan & Mitchell - -	3 lots	Augustine	
3	A. Molinieux - -	1 lot	same	
4	Ann Campbell -	do	same	
5	Frs. Gue - -	do	same	
6	Peter Mitchell -	do	same	
7	Geo. Anderson -	do	same	
8	Robert Isaac - -	3 lots	same	
9	J. M. Hernandez -	1 lot	same	
10	Martin Hernandez -	3 lots	same	
11	J. M. Hernandez -	1 lot	Fernandina	
12	Jos. Bruce - -	do	same	
13	Mag. Villagonga -	do	same	
14	Bruce - -	do	same	
15	Jose Bunnam - -	do	same	
16	Geo. Beassme - -	do	same	
17	Philis Fatio - -	do	same	
18	Jacob Moor - -	do	same	
19	John Mariana - -	do	same	
20	John Moore - -	do	same	
21	Patrica Moore -	do	same	
22	Harry McQueen -	do	same	
23	Clara Mariana - -	do	same	
24	Benjamin Segui -	do	same	
25	Jos. Sanchez - -	do	same	
26	Maria Swelly - -	do	same	
27	Susan Sanchez -	do	same	
28	Torry Travers -	do	same	
29	Torry Travers -	do	same	
30	Mingo Sanco - -	do	same	
31	Jim Rose - -	do	same	
32	Dinana Domingo -	do	same	
33	Bob Robas - -	do	same	
34	Jose Richo - -	do	same	
35	Lucia Valentine -	do	same	
36	Ann Wiggins - -	do	same	
37	Isabella Wiggins -	do	same	
38	Nancy Wiggins -	do	same	

No. 10.—Continued.

No.	Claimants.	Quantity.	City or Town in which the Lots are situated.	Remarks.
39	Nancy Wiggins -	1 lot	Fernandina	
40	John Wright - -	do	same	
41	Vicenti Gill - -	do	same	
42	Ab. Hudson - -	do	same	
43	Heirs of E. Waterman	do	same	
44	Jos. S. Sanchez -	do	same	
45	same - -	do	same	
46	same - -	do	same	
47	same - -	do	same	
48	same - -	do	same	
49	same - -	do	same	

In the above cases the parties have failed to file any evidence of title, and their claims are rejected.

C. DOWNING,
W. H. ALLEN.

REPORT No. 11.

LOTS situated in the "Mil y Quinientas," or 1500 *yards without the gates of St. Augustine.*

NAMES OF		Date of concession.	Quantity of land. Acres.	By whom conceded.	
…nt.	Original claimant.				
	M. Villalonga & J. Hernandez,	July 31, 1811	154 5-6 yards	Estrada	On the left side of the road.
	Thomas de Aguilar,	June 22, 1807	57 yards	White	On the right side of the road.
	Jose Llorente,	June 4, 1807	360¼ yards	White	On the right hand side of the road.
	Pedro Fusha,	Nov. 5, 1801	7	White	Macaris.
	Augustin Tantana,	Aug. 8, 1810	599 1-6 yards	White	Left hand side of the road.
…renzo,	Juan Lorenzo,	June 5, 1807	185 yards	White	Left hand side of the road.
	Jose Barrera,	June 6, 1817	170 yards	Coppinger	Left hand side public road.
	John Gianoply,	June 3, 1807	60½ yards	White	Right hand side of the road.
	Jose Noda,	Feb. 9, 1808	85 yards	White	Right hand side of the road.
	Andrew Pacceti,	May 10, 1807	110 1-6 yards	White	Left hand side of the road.
	John Villalonga,	June 3, 1807	341½ yards	White	Left hand side of the road.
	Pedro Estopa,	July 20, 1807	70½ yards	White	On the right hand side of the road.
	José Garcia,		4	-	On the right hand side of the road.
	Francis Triay,	Oct. 30, 1815	219 yards	Estrada	Left hand side of the road.
	Francis Triay,	June 4, 1807	277 yards	White	Left hand side of the road.
	José Baya,	July 17, 1807	281 5-6 yards	White	Left hand side of the road.
	Francisco Arnau,	June 3, 1807	158 yards	White	Right hand side of the road.
	John Gonzalez,	June 3, 1807	260 yd's 30 inch.	White	Right hand side of the road.
	Bartoleme Lopez,	June 3, 1807	58½ yards	White	Left hand side of the road.
	John Andrew.	July 19, 1820	1	Coppinger	Right hand side of the road.

…ll granted in the same manner and under the same conditions, to wit: That they should revert to the Government whenever … defence of the place. As, we presume that the present Government will never need them for the purposes specified, we re… …f the United States be relinquished, in each case, to the several claimants.

C. DOWNING, *Register,*
W. H. ALLEN, *Receiver.*

REPORT No. 12

Of the cases of George I. F Clarke, &c.

No. 1.

GEORGE I. F. CLARKE, *Claimant*—2000 *acres land.*

The grant is said to have been made by Governor Kindelan, on the memorial of claimant, stating his many services; and, as a further inducement, "that he had no pay, stipend, or other pecuniary aid from the Government, for four years." He prays for 2000 acres; one thousand in 12 mile Swamp, bounded by the lands of Charles and George Clarke, and one thousand in the Hammock called Chacala, which bounds Payne's Savannah on the West.

The decree of Governor Kindelan, in July 1814, is this—That being aware of the services of the petitioner, and the sovereign will, "*requires that good subjects should be rewarded.*" The petition is granted. Now the "*Sovereign Will,*" which grants the power to reward good subjects, is dated in March, 1815, nearly one year after this grant.

It is Thomas Aguilar's certificate alone—we reject it.

No. 2.

GEORGE I. F. CLARKE, *Claimant*—2000 *acres land.*

This tract is divided—one thousand acres is situated in Cedar Hammock, South of Mizelle's Lake, and one thousand acres at the head of Deep Creek. In his memorial to this Board, the claimant states, "The grant was made for services rendered Government." The Governor's decree is dated 16th February, 1811.

If this grant is for services, it is too early by four years. The royal order authorizing their reward in land, bears date 1815. If it is made for head rights, cultivation and occupancy should be proved; which is not done. Let it be remembered, that in the preceding grant in 1814, and this is dated in 1811, he states that he had received no pay, stipend, or other pecuniary aid from the Government, for four years.

This, too, is Aguilar's certificate—rejected.

No. 3.

GEORGE I. F. CLARKE, *Claimant*—4,500 *acres land—Tallahassee and Chacala Hammock.*

This is a part of a grant made to George I. F. Clarke, by Governor Coppinger, as appears by the certificate of Juan de Estralgo, on 17th December, 1817, for services. Clarke sold of this tract 2000 acres, to Estralgo, to whom that portion was recommended for confirmation by the former Board of Land Commissioners, on 6th July, 1824. This part must abide the fate of the other.

No. 4.

George I. F. Clarke, *Claimant—4000 acres land.*

No. 5.

Elias B. Gould, *Claimant—500 acres land.*

No. 6.

Simington, Forbes, and Smith, *Claimants—1500 acres land.*

No. 7.

Thomas Massier, *Claimant—1000 acres land.*

These three claims are a part of No. 4.

This tract is divided, in the petition of the claimant, into three parts, 1000 acres at a place called Spring Garden, on the West side of Lake George. One thousand on the river Hillsborough, at a place called M'Dougall's old plantation. Two thousand acres at the big bend of Derbin's Swamp. The original decree is presented to the Board, of date 3d May, 1816, and two respectable witnesses, Perpall and Alverez, depose positively to their belief, that the decree and signature are in the hand writing of Coppinger. The witnesses had frequently seen the Governor write, and we have no doubt the claim is genuine. The consideration is for services, and as those of Mr. Clarke were notoriously many and meritorious, we have no hesitation in recommending this claim for confirmation.

Of this land, 500 acres in Derbin Swamp have been sold to E. B. Gould, who has presented his claim to this Board, and the sam equantity to Simington, Forbes, and Smith, so as to make up the tract of 2000 acres in that place: 1000 acres at M'Dougalls has been sold to Thomas Napier, and 1000 acres at the Big Spring Still, belongs to the grantee. We consider it as one integral grant, and beyond our final jurisdiction; it is, therefore, recommended. These lands were surveyed in 1819, by Andrew Burgevin.

No. 8.

George I. F. Clarke, *Claimant—4000 acres land.*

Nos. 9 & 10.

M'Intosh and Clinch, *Claimants—2000 acres land.*

No. 11.

Thomas Napier, *Claimant—1000 acres land.*

Parts of No. 8.

On the 10th June, 1816, Charles W. Clarke having petitioned Governor Coppinger for this quantity of land, "for services," the Governor decrees accordingly. The original is before the Board, and proved to be genuine by two respectable witnesses, well acquainted with the Governor's hand writing. The land lies on Chachara hammock, and has been surveyed. Two thousand acres of this land has been sold to General McIntosh and Colonel Duncan Clinch, the first of whom has since transferred it to Geo. J. F. Clarke. The said George has purchased the balance of his brother Charles, and of the whole, he has conveyed to Thomas Napier 1000 acres. The present claimants are all before the Board, for their separate tracts, but we consider it an integral grant, and beyond our jurisdiction to confirm. As it is evidently a genuine grant, we recommend it for confirmation.

No. 12,	Wm. Garvin,	3,000	*Acres.*
13,	Thomas Napier,	1,000	"

Garvin, in 1817, prays a grant in absolute property, of 3,000 acres of land, 2,000 on the Indian River, at a place called Flounder Creek, and 1,000 on Youngblood's Hammock

The original memorial and decree is presented to the Board, and proved to be genuine by two respectable witnesses. The land is granted for losses and services. One thousand acres of that on Indian River is claimed before the Board by Thomas Napier, who is a purchaser of Garvin. The title of the United States is relinquished.

No 14,	Geo. J. F. Clarke,	350	*Acres.*
15,	McDowell & Clarke,	450	"
16,	C. & Geo. Clarke,	1,000	"
17,	James Clarke,	300	"
18,	Duncan L. Clinch,	500	"
19,	Charles & Geo. Clarke,	1,000	"

These claims are subdivided parts of a claim of Honoria Clark, the widow of Thomas Clarke. Thomas Clarke had obtained several grants of land from the British Government here, and had purchased some of other grantees. In 1787, Florida having then become a Spanish province, and Thomas Clarke dead, the widow proceeded to consummate her titles by application to the Spanish Governor Zespodes for their recognition. In her memorial to the Governor she presented nine documents, which, together with the memorial accompanying them, was placed before the Secretary of the Government for his report. The three first were evidences of titles to the lots in this city, with which we have no concern. The other six are as follows, viz:

No. 4. 300 acres of land on the western bank of the Mantanzas, 2½ miles northwest of the fort called Worcester, granted to Thomas Clarke in 1770.

No. 5. 500 acres of land 16 miles south of this city, granted in 1780, called Holmes, to the widow Honoria Clarke.

No. 6. 300 acres near Pablo Creek, granted in 1775.

No. 7. 700 acres on the Middle Creek of Nassau.

No. 8. 500 acres on the Twelve Mile Swamp, now the property of Duncan Clinch; was granted in 1769 to William Penn, and by him sold to Thomas Clarke.

No. 9. 300 acres East of Pablo Creek.

No. 9 was given to the widow Honoria by a direction of Governor Tonyn to the Surveyor General to measure off to her that quantity of land at the place specified. The Secretary Howard reported that this property, from Nos. 4 to 9, inclusive, belonged, from the documents presented, to the widow Honoria Clarke.

In 1792, Mrs. Clarke represented to Governor Quesada that the lands which she owned, on Nassau, 700 acres, and on Pablo Creek, 600 acres, "were so encroached on by neighbors, and it was so difficult, from the removal of the British settlers, to ascertain the lines, that she was willing to relinquish them to the Government, if the Government would grant to her the same quantity on Julington Creek." The Governor, on a favorable report of the Comptroller of the Royal Domain, authorizes the transfer, and directs the survey to be made by Don Pedro Marrot on Julington Creek,

In 1815, Thomas Aguilar certified, that, in the memorial of Honoria Clarke, in 1792, praying a grant of 1,000 acres, for head rights, at the following places, to-wit:

300 acres on the south side of Emery Creek, at Mantanzas.

300 acres at a place called Johnson's Old Plantation, near to Francis Pellicer's

400 acres in a hammock, between Derbin's swamp, and the twenty mile house, on the road to the Bluff. That the Governor made the grant; and decreed the survey, "as soon as convenient."

The survey does not appear on the list of Marrot, in 1801. But, in the titles and positions of Buyck and Dupont, in 1792 and 1801, 2 and 5, the land of Mrs. Clark, on the Mantanzas, are referred to as boundary lines to the grant. So seem to stand these titles, until 1801, when Honoria Clark represented to Governor White, that the land on Julington creek, 1,300 acres, were occupied previously to her exchange, authorized in 1792; and those on Emery's creek, 300 acres, were too much inundated for cultivation; wherefore she prays for 1,600 acres of land on Graham's swamp, at the head of Mantanzas river. Governor White authorized the survey, and directed that she be furnished from the Secretary's Office, with "a certified copy of the memorial and decree, which will serve her as a copy in form;" this last is a genuine document. Some time after the death of Mrs. H. Clarke, her property was divided amongst her heirs, a copy of which division is filed before us, from the record.

The testimony before the Board is solely in reference to the grant of 1,000 acres, made, as certified by Aguilar, by Quesada, in 1792, "for *head rights.*" It is this Francis Pellicer swears, that C. W. Clarke, the son of Honoria, has been, for many years, and is now, in the cultivation of a tract of land on Emery Creek, Mantanzas river; which he understands to be a part of this grant. Joseph S. Sanchez swears, that "the land *at Emery's* creek, has been cultivated and possessed by claimants, for more than fifteen years." So stand the document and testimony, in these cases; cases which have given us more trouble to understand and elucidate, than any other in the office.

To the lands granted by the British Government to Thomas Clarke, and Honoria his widow, and to those under whom they claim, as purchasers, the Clarkes have an undoubted title. The British grantees were required, in 1787, to submit their claims to the Government, and obtain a confirmation. Mrs. Clarke has done so; and, on her title to Nos. 4, 5, 6, 7, 8, and 9, the decision of the Secretary, sanctioned as it was by the Spanish Government, is conclusive; Nos, 6 and 9, 300 acres each, on Pablo creek, and No. 7, 700 acres on the River Nassau, she exchanged in 1792 with Government for the same quantity on the Julington creek; and, subsequently, in 1801, adding to the 1,300 acres on Julington, 300 of a grant on Emery's creek, (part of 1,000 for head rights,) she petitioned and obtained leave to locate the whole 1,600, to wit: 1,300 on Julington, and 300 on Emery's creek, on Graham's swamp.

No. 4, Of the document presented to Secretary Howard, to wit: 300 acres, called Worcester, on Mantanzas.

No. 5, Of the same document, to wit: 500 acres at a place called Holmes; and,

No. 8, 500 acres on the Twelve Mile swamp, now claimed by Colonel Duncan L. Clinch, already alluded to in this report, are based upon valid British grants, recognized by the Spanish Government, and are valid.

Mrs. Clarke, though a British subject, took the necessary oaths of allegiance to Spain, remained in the country; and the many acts of the Spanish Government, already alluded to, show that her claims were recognized as good; and we so consider them.

Nos. 6, 7, 8, and 9, of lands on Nassau river, and Pablo creek; and were exchanged, and abandoned, for 1,300 acres on Graham's swamp. This exchange was made by Gov. Quesada first, and Governor White afterwards.

The title to the 1,300 acres of land on Graham's swamp is valid; but the parties claim 300 acres more, under the same title, by exchange, for the 300 relinquished on Emery's creek.

It should be remembered, that this on Emery's creek, is a part of 1,000 acres, claimed as a donation to Mrs. Clarke in 1792, of which there is no direct evidence, but the certificate of Aguilar. Such a certificate, if unaided by collateral proof, we can never recognise. The best evidence that the grant was made, is to be found in the memorial of Mrs. Clarke in 1801, to permit her to exchange lands, a part of which are these very 300 acres on Emery's creek, proved nowhere to be granted, but by the certificate aforesaid, and the authority given by Governor White to do so. Take away this grant by exchange in 1801, to lands in Derbin Swamp, and we should have no hesitation in rejecting this claim of 1,000 acres; as it stands, with the evidence before the Board, that these lands were divided among the heirs of Honoria Clarke in 1806, and that division recognised as valid, and admitted to record, taken too in connexion with the testimony of Sanchez and Pellicer, we have no doubt that the grant was made in 1792, and conceded by Governor White in 1801, as the property of Mrs. Clarke. It at the same time appears to us, that Mrs. Clarke did not abandon Emery's creek, as she had proposed; and that she is not entitled to the 300 acres in Derbin's swamp, which her representatives claim, as obtained in its place. In 1806, Emery's tract was divided amongst the heirs of Mrs. Clarke. In 1828, the evidence is, that the place has been cultivated fifteen years back.

They cannot, therefore, claim the 300 acres in Derbin's Swamp, and still hold possession of Emery's Tract, which was tendered by Mrs. Clarke in exchange for it. For these reasons, we confirm to Mrs. Honoria Clarke's representatives, the 1000 acres granted in 1792 for head rights, and divided into three tracts, as above described, and 1300 acres only in Derbin's Swamp.

In our decision on these cases, it will be seen that the numbers which we have used, refer to the document presented by Honoria Clarke, and not *to the* No. on this report.

No. 20.

Geo. J. F. Clarke, *Claimant—2000 acres land.*

Thomas Aguilar's certificate is dated the 13th January. 1812. There is no original in the office of Public Archives. It is to this effect, that, in the memorial of George J. F. Clarke, of the same month and year, stating that Governor White had granted him 2000 acres of land in Derbin's swamp, for his services during the years 1797 and 9, he had found those lands not suitable to his purpose, and prays that he may locate the grant at a place called Yellowsasse, which is an orange grove, situated West of the river St. John's, and South of the road to Panton Leslie's store." Estrado decreed the exchange. It is strange, if this grant was ever made, that the original, by White, cannot be found. It should be remembered that the Royal order, authorizing grants of lands for services, is dated in 1815, and this certificate in 1812, one year after Governor White's death. The claim is rejected. *See No.* 1 *of this report, where the claimant declares, in* 1814, *that he had received "no pay, stipend, or reward, for four years."*

No. 21.

C. W. Clarke, *Claimant*—375 *acres.*

This is a petition in 1815, for 500 acres of land as head rights. Estraldo, the acting Governor, decides that he is entitled to only 375. Aguilar's certificate of these facts, is dated in the same year. There is no evidence of occupancy. It is rejected.

No. 22.

C. W. Clarke, *Claimant*—300 *acres land.*

Aguilar certifies that Coppinger granted claimant 300 acres of land on the East side of Lake George, for agriculture and the raising of stock, in 1817. There is an affidavit taken in this case, of too general a nature to benefit the claimant; it is, "that the country, from the revolutions and invasions of the province, was in that state of troubles and fears, which went to deter settlement in the unprotected part thereof." A man has no right to ask for land incumbered with condition of settlement, when he knows he cannot settle it. It is at his price. If he chooses to settle it, and run the hazard, he may; but he cannot give as a reason for not performing a condition implied, a fact which he knew, at the same time, would prevent the performance. In any event, it does not cure the defect of Aguilar's certificate. It is rejected.

No. 23.

C. W. Clarke, *Claimant*—1,576 *acres.*

No. 24.

Richard Weightman, *Claimant*—200 *acres.*

No. 25.

Andrew Stores, *Claimant*—500 *acres.*

No. 26.

C. W. Clarke, *Claimant*—2300 *acres.*

No. 27.

Daniel Clarke, *Claimant*—500 *acres.*

No. 28.

JAMES CLARKE, *Claimant*—500 *acres.*

No. 29.

THOMAS CLARKE. *Claimant*—500 *acres.*

No. 26 is another of Aguilar's eternal certificates, of which No. 23. 24 and 25, are portions.

In the memorial to this Board, Clarke says the land was divided as follows, to wit :

800 acres on the East side of Lake George.
404 do. at same place.
292 do. at same place.
200 do. sold to Richard Weightman, situated at the same place.
500 do. sold to Andrew Stores.

All these tracts, except the two last, are said to have been surveyed, and we are favored with the metes and bounds.

By the certificate of Aguilar, already mentioned, it appears that this land was granted by concession, for services in 1817.

Nos. 27, 28, and 29, are all grants for services, dated on the 18th December, 1817, and located in Twelve Mile Swamp, evidenced by Aguilar's certificate, the original of which is not to be found.

The evidence in claim No. 26, of which Nos. 23, 24, and 25, are component parts, is this : George I. F. Clark, the brother of the claimant, deposes, that, at the suggestion of the Governor, made to the deponent, the said Charles W. Clark would get more land; deponent wrote a petition for claimant, presented it, and understood from the Governor that it would be granted. The evidence in claims Nos. 27, 28, and 29, is the oath of the same party, G. Clark, the father of the three claimants, "that Governor Coppinger having spontaneously expressed to me his sense of the services of these men, and his desire to give each of them a tract of land, witness wrote claimant's memorial, and handed them to the Governor, who passed them over to his Secretary, Aguilar, for *their decrees;* and that he, witness, afterwards received from Aguilar the certified copies now before the Board." As these claims of his brother and sons, depend solely upon the evidence of Mr Clark, we take pleasure in saying, from our knowledge of his character, that, notwithstanding his relationship to the parties, we place implicit reliance on his statement, and confirm the four claims above.

No. 30.

GEORGE I. F. CLARKE, *Claimant*—1000 *acres in the Big Savannah, at Mantanzas.*

A grant, as Aguilar certifies, made in 1801, for cattle grazing. There is no proof, and the claim is rejected.

C. DOWNING,
W. H. ALLEN.

Nos.	Names of — Present Claimants.	Names of — Original Claimants.	Date of Concession, or Order of Survey.	Quantity of Land. Acres.
1	George J. F. Clarke -	George J. F. Clarke -	July, 1814	2,000
2	Same - -	Same - -	16 Feb. 1811	2,000
3	Same - -	Same - -	17 Dec. 1817	4,500
4	Same - -	Same - -	3 May, 1816	4,000
5	Elias B. Gould -	Same - -	-	500
6	Simonton -	Same - -	-	1,500
7	Thomas Napier -	Same - -	-	1,000
8	Charles W. Clarke -	Charles W. Clarke -	10 June, 1816	4,000
9 & 10	Gen. McIntosh and Col. Clinch - -	Same - -	-	2,000
11	Thomas Napier -	Same - -	-	1,000
12	William Garvin -	William Garvin -	1817	3,000
13	Thomas Napier -	Same - -	-	1,000
14	George J. F. Clarke -	Honoria Clarke -	-	350
15	McDowell & Black -	Same - -	-	450
16	Charles & Geo. Clarke	Same - -	-	1,000
17	James Clarke -	Same - -	-	300
18	Duncan Clinch -	Same - -	-	500
19	Charles & Geo. Clarke	Same - -	1801	1,000
20	George J. F. Clarke -	George J. F. Clarke -	13 Jan. 1812	2,000
21	Charles W. Clarke -	Charles W. Clarke -	1815	375
22	Same - -	Same - -	1817	300
23	Same - -	Same - -	-	1,576
24	Richard Weightman -	C. W. Clarke - -	-	200
25	Andrew Stores -	C. W. Clarke - -	-	500
26	Charles W. Clarke -	C. W. Clarke - -	1817	2,300
27	Daniel Clarke -	Daniel Clarke -	18 Dec. 1817	500
28	James Clarke -	James Clarke -	18 Dec. 1817	500
29	Thomas Clarke -	Thomas Clarke -	18 Dec. 1817	500
30	George J. F. Clarke -	Geo. J. F. Clarke -	1801	1,000

Continued.

By whom Conceded.	Authority, or royal order, underwhich the concession was granted	Conditions.	Situation.	General Remarks.
Kindelan -	1815 -	None	12 mile Swamp & Chachala Hammoc - -	Aguilar's Certificate. Rejected.
White -	1815 -	"	Cedar Hammoc & Deep Creek - - -	Ditto. do Rejected.
Coppinger	-	"	Talahassee and Chachala Hammoc - -	This is part of a grant, the balance of which was recommended for confirmation by B. L. C.
Coppinger	-	"	Spring Grove, Hillsboro' & Durbin's Swamp	
-	-	-	Durbin Swamp - -	These three claims are portions of No. 4, sold to present claimants by the grantee, Clark, and are all recommended for confirm'n.
-	-	-	Durbin Swamp - -	
-	-	-	McDougal - -	
Coppinger	1815 -	-	Chachala Hammoc.	These are parts of No. 8, and are recommended for confirmation.
-	-	-	Same - -	
-	-	-	Same - -	
Coppinger	1815 -	-	Indian River and Young Blood's Hammoc -	Confirmed.
-	-	-	Indian River - -	A part of No. 12.
-	-	-		Subdivided parts of land confirmed by the Spanish Gov'nt to Honoria Clarke, originally granted by the British. See rep. confirm'd.
-	-	-		
-	-	-		
-	-	-		
-	-	-	12 Mile Swamp - -	
White -	1790 -	-	Matanzas - -	Confirmed.
Estrada -	For services	-	Orange grove, West of St. John's River -	Rejected.
Estrada -	1790 -	-	Dunn's Lake - -	Rejected.
Coppinger	1815 -	-	East side of Lake George	Rejected.
-	-	-	Situated on the East side of Lake George -	This is a part of No. 26 that follows. Recommended for confirmation.
-	-	-	Ditto ditto	These are parts of No. 26. Recommended for confirmation.
Coppinger	1815 -	-	Ditto ditto	Recommended for confirmation.
"	" -	-	12 Mile Swamp -	Confirmed.
"	" -	-	Ditto - -	Confirmed.
"	" -	-	Ditto - -	Confirmed.
White -	-	-	At the Big Savannah, Matanzas. - -	For cattle grazing Rejected.

C. DOWNING,
W. H. ALLEN.

REPORT No. 13.

LIST OF CLAIMS in which no Title of Property has been filed.

Numbers.	Names.	No. of acres.	Papers filed.
1	Absalom Beardon and wife	150	
2	Daniel Brockington -	200	
3	Spicer Christopher -	500	We suppose this land the same confirmed to his ancestor.
4	John M. Carter - -	100	
5	Heirs of Andrew Dewees	1,809½	
6	Horatio S. Dexter - -	Alachua.	
7	H. S. Dexter & John Grace	3 miles sq.	
8	Horatio S. Dexter - -	2,000	This is a part of a grant to J. F. Rattenbury, made after date, and rejected by B. L. C.
9	Thos. C. Doremus - -	500	
10	J. Drysdale and J. Rodman	2,262	This is a part of Alachua, recommended for confirmation by B. L. C.
11	Joseph Delespine - -	200	
12	James Darley - -	500	Plat and certificate of survey.
13	Stephen Eubanks - -	256	Concession since filed, and reported at length in Report 2, No. 120.
14	William Frink - -	321	
15	Isaac Frost - -	1,500	
16	Do - - -	2,000	
17	The executor of J. Frazer	3,000	
18	Domingo Fernandez -	322	
19	E. Fallis - - -	mill seat	Deed of bargain and sale.
20	Robert Gilbert - -	200	
21	Do - -	300	
22	John Gennings - -	250	
23	Wm. Hollingsworth -	250	
24	Mary Hayden - -	250	
25	Isaac Hendricks - -	450	
26	William Lane - -	300	Affidavit of Samuel Wilson.
27	William Lain - -	300	
28	Do - -	100	
29	William Lane - -	400	
30	Geo. Long - -	300	The papers in these two claims have been brought in, and six hundred acres confirmed. See Report 1, No. 77.
31	The heirs of Geo. Long -	350	
32	John McClure - -	900	
33	Manuel Marshall - -	250	
34	Heirs of John McQueen -	10,000	
35	Heirs of Wm. Mills, jr. -	500	
36	Jane Miers - - -	200	
37	William Monroe - -	300	
38	Heirs of Geo. Morrison -	indefinite.	
39	James Plummer - -	265	Plat and certificate of survey.
40	Daniel Plummer - -	600	
41	Heirs of Isaac Revaz -	4,000	Affidavit of Edward Wanton.
42	Heirs of James Richard -	200	
43	Samuel Russel, sen. -	300	
44	James Suydam, - -	500	
45	Anthony Suarez - -	500	
46	Philip Solona - -	100	
47	William Thomas - -	200	Affidavit of John Hall, and conveyance.
48	Heirs of Geo. Taylor -	Casacolo.	Claimed to be the same land decided on, Report 1, No. 23.

LIST—Continued.

Numbers.	Names.	No. of acres.	Papers filed.
49	Heirs of George Taylor, -	Punta del cano de san Pablo.	
50	Do do -	64	
51	Do do -	"Surra de Agua," water saw-mill.	
52	George Tillet - -	undefined.	
53	John Uptegrove - -	100	
54	James Woodland - -	200	Two deeds of sale.
55	John Williamson - -	850	
56	Robt. Walker's administrator	100	
57	Joseph F. White - -	200	

In all of the above cases, with the exception of Nos. 30 and 31, there has been filed by the parties no evidence of title, and they are therefore *all* rejected.

C. DOWNING,
W. H. ALLEN.

REPORT No. 14.

A report on conflicting British and Spanish grants.

No. 1.

William Thomas Jones, *Claimant*—2000 *acres of land.*

This is a British grant, made by Governor James Grant, on the 12th January, 1770, to Abraham Jones, the ancestor of the present claimant. There is a survey properly certified, and an endorsement on the back of the grant, that it was registered in January, 1770.

The land lies in the fork of Maxton's, now M'Girt's Creek, and the River St. John. Much testimony has been filed in the case, all of which amounts to this: That, when this Province was transferred by the British to the Spanish Government, in 1763, Abraham Jones, the grantee, being then dead, all his family, with the exception of his son William, removed to the State of Georgia. William, then a minor by the laws of Spain, remained in the city of St. Augustine, an apprentice to a trade. The treaty between Spain and Great Britain was signed in January, 1783, and ratified by the King of Spain in September following. In May, 1783, William Jones' brothers signed a deed to him for the land in question, conveying to him all the right and title which they might possess thereto. The deed further specifies, that William intends to remain in Florida; and by the direction of their father's will, his lands should belong to either of his sons who should continue to reside in the Province It is uncertain at what time William abandoned his residence in this place. It appears from the testimony before us, that, in 1794 or 1795, he removed to the State of Georgia, and continued there until his death in 1814. Whether he remained in the Province until his settlement in Georgia, we have no means of deciding.

The above is a succinct abstract, embracing, as we believe, all the important points contained in the voluminous testimony before us, from William Jones; the title to the present claimant is regularly deduced.

No. 2.

John H. M'Intosh, *Claimant*—3,274 *acres of land.*

This is as good a Spanish title as can be made; and, if there was no conflicting British claim, we should have no hesitation in confirming it. As it is, it becomes our duty to report the evidence of title to Congress.

It covers the land claimed by Jones in the preceding number of this report. It lies between the River St. John and M'Girt's, once Maxon's, Creek. The title is as follows: In 1792, a survey, under the direction of Pedro Marrot, of 98 cavallerias and eight acres (3,274 acres); and, on the 27th February, 1804, a Royal title, made by Governor White, to John M'Queen, to whom it had been first surveyed and conceeded; and, in March, same year, a sale by M'Queen to the present claimant, duly authorized and recorded.

CHAS. DOWNING,
W. H. ALLEN.

REPORT No. 14. *On conflicting British and Spanish Grants.*

NAMES OF		Date of the Grant.	Quantity of land.	By whom conceded.	Situation.
...ant.	Original Claimant.		Acres.		
...nes -	Abraham Jones -	Jan. 12, 1770	2,000	Grant	Maxton's or M'Girt's Cr.
...osh -	John M'Queen -	Feb. 27, 1804	3,274	White	St. John's River.

No. 15.

A report of 16 claims, omitted on the abstracts of the Land Commissioners, and transmitted to us by the Commissioner of the General Land Officers.

No. 1.

W. J. Fatio, and others, *Claimants*—720 *acres of land.*

This claim was confirmed by the Commissioners, on the 12th October, 1824. It was a mistake in the Department, to transmit it to us, with those which follow. It is the 3d claim on report No. 6, of 29th December, 1824. and has been confirmed by Congress.

No. 2.

Francis P. Sanchez, *Claimant*—800 *acres of land.*

Sanchez purchased this land of Joseph Maria Agarte, to whom it was conceded by Coppinger, for services, in December, 1817. It was surveyed by Burgevin, at a place called Alligator creek, and at another place called Funk's Savannah, in February, 1821. 350 acres were laid off at the first place, and 450 acres at the second. The decree of confirmation is dated 10th June, 1824.

No. 3.

Bernardo Segui, *Claimant*—7000 *acres of land.*

This grant was made by Estrado to the claimant, on the 20th December, 1815, surveyed by Burgevin on the 10th September, 1818, and recommended for confirmation on the 20th January, 1824. It lies on the East side of the St. John's river, at a place known as Buffalo Bluffs.

No. 4.

Wm. Williams's heirs, *Claimants*—2020 *acres of land.*

No. 5.

180 *acres of land.*

In 1803, Williams having proved to the satisfaction of Governor White, by the report of the Engineer, that, under the royal order of 1790, he was entitled as a new settler to 2200 acres of land, they were granted to him at Smyrna.

In 1804, having discovered that the lands at the place were sterile, and the location sickly, he applied for, and obtained leave to locate 2020 acres.

a part of the grant, on the St. John's river, on a creek called "Spring Garden. "The mouth of the aforementioned creek forming the survey," reserving at the same time, 180 acres of the first location, to cover the buildings which he had already erected. The evidence in this case, to wit: the testimony of Summerrall and Dexter, is already before the Department at Washington. It was confirmed on the 1st October, 1824.

No. 6.

NICHOLAS RODRIGUEZ, *Claimant—300 acres land.*

Quesada conceded this land to Lorenzo Rodriguez, in February, 1793. On the death of Lorenzo, Nicholas, the son, became the purchaser; and the petition and sale of Lorenzo was confirmed by an official act of the Spanish Government, on the 18th September, 1816. The land was confirmed to the present claimant, by the Board of Land Commissioners, on the 11th September, 1824. It is situated on Anastatia Island, at a place called Buena Vista, and on a creek called, *Cano de la Escelta,* near the light-house.

No. 7.

GEORGE ATKINSON, *Claimant—550 acres land.*

All the papers in this claim were copied at large by the former Board of Commissioners, and sent on to Washington. They are shortly these; in 1816, George Clarke having surveyed the land in the preceding year, Gov. Coppinger granted to Atkinson, 550 acres of land, on the North side of the river St. Johns, by a royal title. Atkinson was a new settler, and obtained the land under the order of 1790. This claim, as was suggested by a note endorsed at the Department, is on the abstract of 1824, No. 26, of report No. 1. It is there registered in the name of Francis P. Sanchez, which is a mistake; Sanchez has no such claim, and the date of the survey, and of the grant, as well as the location and boundaries of the land, prove the identity of the claim, and the misnomer of the claimant on the abstract. It was confirmed on the 11th June, 1824.

No. 8.

ANTONIO ALVEREZ, *Claimant—1500 acres of land.*

This land, on the first memorial of the claimant to the Board, was claimed to be situated on the West side of the Ocktawaha creek, and to have been surveyed there by Andrew Burgevin, "by the authority of the Government," granted to Burgevin for that purpose. By the permission of the Board, he subsequently changed the location of the grant, having perhaps discovered better land upon which to place it. The title to this property has been transmitted to the Department. It was recommended for confirmation on the 8th September, 1824.

No. 9.

SAMUEL CLARKE and GEO. S. BROWN, *Claimants—3000 acres land.*

In April 1798, Thomas Travers, on behalf of the children, then in the United States, of his brother Patrick Travers, deceased, "a subject of his Catholic Majesty," petitioned for 3000 acres of pine land, at a place called Pigeon creek, on the river St. Mary's, "for the purpose of building a water saw mill," and 300 acres of planting land, on Amelia Island, at a place called the Horse-pen. On a favorable report of the Engineer, Governor White conceded the land to the claimant in 1799; Geo. Clarke surveyed it in 1819, and Governor Coppinger, in the same year, issued a royal title. The lands seem to have been regularly conveyed from the grantee to the present claimants. Three witnesses have been sworn in this case, whose testimony is on file in the Department at Washington. They all prove the same fact, that Travers built the mill in compliance with the terms of the grant, and that Clarke and Brown have greatly improved the property. This claim was confirmed by the Board of Commissioners on the 28th December, 1824. We do not know what has heen done with the claim to the 300 acres, at the Horse-pen, on Amelia Island.

No. 10.

WILLIAM TRAVERS, *Claimant—450 acres of land.*

In pursuance of the Royal order of 1790, Gov. White granted to L. Ortega, June, 1798, 450 acres of land, at a place called Santa Lucia, on the North River. It was surveyed by Andrew Burgevin, and sold by Ortega to the present claimant. On the testimony of one witness, that it had been cultivated by Ortega up to May 1821, it was confirmed by the Board of Land Commissioners, on the 30th September, 1824.

No. 11.

W. P. SANCHEZ, *Claimant—100 acres of land.*

In 1797, Gov. White conceded to John Bousquet 200 acres of land, situated on Guana creek, on the North River. In the subsequent year the Gov. permitted the grantee to transfer his claim to John Cavedo and A. Acosta, one half to each. In 1804, it (Acosta's portion) was surveyed and came by regular conveyances to the possession of the present claimant, to whom it was confirmed on the 11th October, 1824.

No. 12.

JOHN B. GAUDRY, *Claimant—1500 acres of land.*

Gaudry claims this land, under a grant made to Don Bartolo de Castro y Perrer, by Gov. Coppinger, on the 9th October, 1817, under the Royal order of 1790. The land is situated at a place called Spring Garden, on the River St. Johns, and was recommended for confirmation on the 21st September, 1824.

No. 13.

FRANCES FARREIRA, *Claimant—Key Bacas.*

The grant to this land was made by Governor Kindelan, in January, 1814, for services. The testimony is filed in the Land Office at Washington. It was recommended for confirmation on the 19th June, 1824.

No. 14.

JOSEPH M. HERNANDEZ, *Claimant—3200 acres of land.*

Hernandez claims this land, as Attorney for his wife, Don Anne Maria Hill, widow of Samuel Williams, to whom it was granted by Royal title, dated the 18th April, 1817, "by virtue of the Royal order of 1790." It is situated in the Territory of Halifax, and was surveyed by John Purcell in 1804.

No. 15.

MICHAEL CROSBY's heirs, *Claimants—for 2000 acres of land.*

It appears by the decree of the Boards in this case, of December, 1824, that Coppinger conceded this land to Michael Crosby on the 24th January, 1818, and issued a Royal title for the same, on the 2d day of March succeeding. It was surveyed by George Clarke on the 12th day of April, 1818. It lies on the West side of the River St. Johns, opposite to a place called Mount Tucker. All the papers in this case are on file in the Land Office at Washington.

No. 16.

MARGARET ACOSTA, *Claimant—34½ yards front of land.*

Acosta laid her claim before the Board of Commissioners for 640 acres of land, under the donation act. That claim was rejected, and 34½ yards front upon the road leading from the gate of the city, and within 500 yards of its fortifications, were confirmed to her. It is a claim similar to those on report No. 11, of this Session. The decree of confirmation bears date the 28th December, 1824.

C. DOWNING.
W. H. ALLEN.

No. 15, of 16 Cases sent back from Washington to the Register and Receiver for their report.

...nts.	Original Claimants.	Date of Royal Title.	Date of Concession.	No. acres of land.	By whom conceded.	Royal order &c.	Situation and Remarks.
...ers -	Francis P. Fatio - -	British title	- -	Resurveyed.	-	1,793	This claim will be found on Report No. 6 of 1824, No 3 on said report.
-	Joseph M. Ugarte -	- -	Dec. 17, 1717	800	Coppinger	1815	Alligator creek 350 & 450 on Funk's Savannah.
-	B. Segui - -	- -	Dec. 20, 1815	7,000	Kindelan	1813-15	Between Dunn's lake and Horse landing.
...s -	Wm. Williams - -	- -	Sep. 6, 1804	2,020	White	1,790	Spring Garden.
-	Same - -	- -	- -	180	White	1,790	Musquitoe.
-	Lorenzo Rodriguez -	- -	Feb. 16, 1793	300	Quesada	1,790	Buena Vista Anastatia Isl'd.
-	George Atkinson -	- -	Feb. 22, 1816	550	Coppinger	1,790	West river, St. Johns'.
-	Antonio Alvererez -	- -	Dec. 7, 1817	1,500	Coppinger	1815	Big Hammock.
...Brown	Thomas Travers -	- -	April, 1798	3,000	White	-	For building a water Saw-mill, St. Mary's river
-	Lazaro Ortega - -	- -	June 4, 1798	450	White	-	Santa Lucia, North river.
-	John Bosquet - -	- -	Aug. 18, 1797	100	White	1,790	North river, Warner creek.
-	Barth. de Castro de Ferrer	- -	Oct. 9, 1817	1,500	Coppinger	1,790	Spring garden, St. Johns' r.
-	Francis Farreira -	- -	Jan. 5, 1814	-	Kindelan	1,790	Key Bacas.
...atty &c.	Samuel Williams -	- -	July 21, 1808	3,200	White	1,790	Halifax river.
...eirs -	Michael Crosby -	March 2, 1818	Jan. 24, 1818	2,000	Coppinger	1,790	West side river St. Johns.
-	Peter Estopa - -	- -	June 3, 1807	341½	yards front	-	Situated out side of the gates.

C. DOWNING,
W. H. ALLEN.

6, *of Claims rejected by the Board of Land Commissioners, and not reported by them to Congress.*

OF Original Claimants.	Date of Royal Title.	Date of Concession.	Quantity of Land. Acres.	By whom Conceded.	Royal Order.	Situation.
Villiam Travers -	5 Nov. 1818	-	1,000	Coppinger -	1815	East of Dunn's lake.
rancisco Rivera -	31 Oct. 1818	-	1,000	Coppinger -	1815	South of Lake George, St. John's river.
rancis P. Sanchez -	31 Oct. 1818	-	1,000	Coppinger -	1815	Head of Indian River.
avid Garvin -	5 Dec. 1814	-	Martin's Isl'd	Kindelan -	1790	Martin's Island, St. Mary's river.
. Wilds - -	-	-	184	-	-	Geo. I. F. Clarke's survey, dated 8th May, 1818, St Mary's river.
ames Woods -	-	-	75	-	-	Geo. I. F. Clarke's survey, dated 13th December, 1818, Mill's swamp.
rederick Hartley -	-	-	400	-	-	Surveyed by Pedro Marrot, 6th March, 1792, on Nassau river.
heop. J. Woods, sen.	-	-	370	-	-	Surveyed by Geo Clarke in two tracts, 9th Nov. 1818, and 10th Dec. 1820.
homas Higginbottom	-	-	200	-	-	Geo. I. F. Clarke's survey, dated 17th Oct. 1818, River St. Mary's.
harles Hovey -	-	-	400	-	-	Geo. I. F. Clarke's survey, dated 18th June, 1821, River Nassau.
tephen Eubanks -	-	-	450	-	-	Geo. I. F. Clarke's survey, dated 17th Dec. 1818, No. of Thomas' Swamp.
axey Dell - -	-	-	700	-	-	Surveyed by Geo. Clarke in two tracts, dated 9th July, 1818, and 18th May, 1818.
rancis R. Sanchez -	-	-	500	-	-	Geo. I. F. Clarke's survey, dated 16th November, 1819, Hog Town creek.
oseph S. Sanchez -	-	-	400	-	-	Geo. I. F. Clarke's survey, dated 8th Dec. 1819, Hog Town creek.

ABSTRACT, No. 16—Continued.

...es of Original Claimants.	Date o Royal Title.	Date of Concession.	Quantity of Land. Acres.	By whom Conceded.	Royal Order.	Situation.
John Sanchez -	-	..	400	-	-	Geo. I. F. Clarke's survey, dated 6th Dec. 1819, Hog Town Creek.
J. F. Rattenbury -	-	26 Feb. 1818	3,500	Coppinger -	-	Volucia, St. John's river.
James Baird -	-	3 Jan. 1812	Undefined.	Estrada -	-	Indian and Jupiter rivers.
Jos. Summerall -	-	7 May, 1817	150	Coppinger -	-	Cormorant Branch, Julington creek.
Lewis Guibert -	-	-	640	-	-	A donation claim.
Seymour Picket -	-	-	640	-	-	Same.
David Scurry -	-	-	640	-	-	Same.
Jesse Carlisle -		-	640	-	-	Same.
Hardy Alanier -	-	-	640	-	-	Same.
William Evins -	-	-	640	-	-	Same.

.bove, the following claims were presented to the Board of Commissioners, and by them rejected, as will appear by the following
nutes, of the 29th March, 1824 :
ritish claims were this day presented to the Board, viz.
nor, for twelve thousand acres of land, situated on the west side of St. John's river;
for twenty thousand acres of land on the East side of Indian river;
o', for twenty thousand acres of land on the East side of St. John's river;
n Berresford, twenty thousand acres on the East side of St John's river;
illiam Berresford, twenty thousand acres on the East side of St. John's river;
:wenty thousand acres on a branch of North Hillsboro' river;
twenty thousand acres on the East side of St. John's river;
s, twenty thousand acres on the Western side of St. John's river;
ord, twenty thousand acres on the East side of St. John's river;
enty thousand acres East side of Lake George;
yn, Esq. for twenty thousand and one hundred and twenty-five acres: the first on the West side of St. John's river, and the last
s creek;
n, for one thousand acres in the twelve-mile swamp;

housand acres on Nassau;
o hundred and fifty acres, head of Rainsford saw-mill creek;
ne hundred acres, head of St. Sebastian creek; one hundred and fifty-eight acres, five miles North of St. Augustine; one
ead of Tolomato river; six hundred and forty acres at Diego Fort; five hundred acres at the forks of Rains Cowpen creek;
ty-six acres at twelve-mile swamp; six hundred and twenty-fives acres on a branch of Nassau river; one town-lot No. 2, on
town lot, No. 3, on Grenville quarter."
ered, that these claims be rejected; the applicants having failed to shew that they are *bona fide* citizens of the United States;
been compensated for these claims by the British Government, from whom they derive title."
of the first of April, 1824, we extract the following:
y presented his memorial to this Board, for two thousand six hundred acres of land, situated in the following manner, viz:
situated on the southern extremity of Jupiter Island; one-sixth part on the point situated to the North thereof, on Indian
aining parts in the wood or swamp in the Southeast part of Lake George, without exhibits; which was, after due considera-
Board."
et al. presented their memorial to this Board, for fifty thousand acres of land in East Florida, without exhibits, which was
."

CHAS. DOWNING,
W. H. ALLEN.

www.ingramcontent.com/pod-product-compliance
Lightning Source LLC
Chambersburg PA
CBHW080240270326
41926CB00020B/4316